STRUCTURED

DECISION

MAKING

For Managing Work and Life

Edward M. Collins, PhD

ISBN: 1-4392-3317-9
ISBN-13: 9781439233177
Library of Congress Control Number: 2009902574

Visit www.booksurge.com to order additional copies.

Contents

Preface

Everything should be made as simple as possible, but not simpler.

Albert Einstein

That thought has guided the preparation of this book. It is both short and as long as it needs to be. Its purpose is to provide the potential for a significant early improvement in decision making and continued development over a lifetime. Its major premise: decisions are not only management's principal product, but also the decisive function in managing all human activity. It provides a structured decision making process proven by long usage and applicable equally to managing oneself, one's career and life, and - if one's existing or prospective career is management - one's organization. It then examines the factors that influence decision making for good or ill, drawing upon the whole body of human experience and thought with respect to both individual and group decision makers.

Chapter 1

On Decisions and Decision Making

DECISIONS AND LIFE

The Early Years

An infant child, let us say a girl, emerges from the darkness of a mother's womb into the unfamiliar light of the delivery room and of the world. The giants in the delivery room promptly administer various indignities necessary to her health, such as a thorough cleanup, removing the mucous from her respiratory system, treating her eyes, severing the lifeline that has supported her these many months. Within seconds of her emergence, this infant has received and absorbed some information, concluded that this is no way to treat a lady when she enters a room, and informed the surrounding giants of her displeasure via an unmistakable cry of protest. She has made and acted upon the first of the millions of decisions which will shape and define her life.

Her mother names her Wilhelmina, in honor of the mother's childless, slightly eccentric, greatly loved, but also very rich old great-aunt. Her father shares the hope that the name will bring his daughter a rich inheritance, and proposes that she be called Billie, a feminine form of the Bill that he had hoped for. The mother wants some rest and recuperation before pondering that matter.

Several decisions that may significantly affect her life having already been made, or identified and deferred, Wilhelmina's path to adult life will then be guided by decisions made by others: what to eat, when to eat, what to wear, when to sleep, when to awake, what to believe and place in her mind as lasting guidance, what schools to attend and what subjects to take, what to do and what not to do. The quality of her life will depend upon those decisions until she reaches adolescence and begins to define herself as a person and assert her desire, her right and necessity, to take over by degrees the making of decisions regarding her life. Her parents, older relatives, and teachers will have, for good or ill, done much to shape her character and education, which will in turn influence her decisions. Ordinarily, her elders will have done nothing directly to teach her how to make important decisions, how to manage her life.

Our hypothetical young lady, entering the usually difficult and often dangerous path which leads from childhood and dependence to adulthood and independence, is substantially the model for all of us. Most of us have had loving parents, older relatives, and dedicated teachers who have guided us by their experience and thought, and most older persons have similarly guided their own children, younger relatives, and students. This is, I believe, a natural and necessary process for the years between birth and adolescence, when parental love and experience and the accumulated wisdom - or lack thereof - of a particular culture must be imparted to protect the immature child from destructive behavior, or perhaps behavior offensive to her cultural milieu. In our early years we are taught a set of beliefs intended as a guide to our actions. As adults, most of us follow the same path in the intellectual and moral development of our children. We do that in the hope of shielding the inexperienced and developing child from bad decisions. But, one cannot give what one does not have, and most of us have little training or education that directly addresses decision-making as a process that can be beneficially ordered and structured. We teach *what to do, what not to do*, much more than we teach how to decide *what to do, what not to do*. Our primary and secondary school systems, and society at large, similarly teach codes of behavior, but do not include decision making in their curricula.

That situation seems incongruous. Decisions are as common in human life as hydrogen in the universe. Each of us, every day, makes hundreds of them, from the time we decide to get up in the morning until we decide to go to bed, and sometimes during waking periods when we ought to be, and wish we were, sleeping. In a very real sense, then, life is a succession of decisions. Although chance and the flow of events play important roles, the success or failure of human endeavors, public or private, rest heavily upon the quality of their decisions. Most of those are very ordinary and of no particular importance by themselves, but cumulatively even our small decisions influence what we are, what we will become, how we appear to others, what success and happiness we may achieve in life, even how we define success and happiness. Occasionally, of course, we must make decisions which will have very significant influences. One can therefore state with high confidence that bad decisions make for bad lives, good decisions for good lives. Decision-making constitutes the essence of the management of one's life and one's work and career: everyone, regardless of occupation, is perforce the "manager" of one's own life, and everyone may therefore benefit from a substantial dose of decision making theory and practice. As Aristotle put it, "the manner of a man's life is a clue to what he on reflection regards as the good - in other words, happiness."[1]

The professional manager has a large additional obligation: making decisions that affect human affairs, human organizations, individual people, in increasing numbers at increasingly higher levels of management. I hold, elsewhere and throughout this book, that "management" and decision-making are so closely related that one may think of them as, if not the same thing, inseparable. So, this is a book about decision making as the centerpiece of managing one's work and life.

The Path and Price of Success

I assert elsewhere that every human decision rests upon the desired consequences outweighing the undesired. Accordingly, I accept here the obligation to identify some things you will not gain by reading this book, and some that I believe you will. First, I do not offer the book as the Rosetta Stone of decision making and/or managerial success. It contains nothing that has not been found useful by long practice. It offers nothing that would merit being called profound: some of the measures it describes could reasonably be regarded as useful "trade craft." It is intended to inform rather than entertain. It will not take you directly to the top level of decision making skills, but it offers potential for immediate improvement and may show you a path for continuing development. If your career lies or will lie in management as a profession, it may serve as a constant reminder that development as a manager is an inseparable part of one's total personal development. If you are already well advanced in your professional life, it may remind you of how quickly and how far you may fall, and what the common causes of rapid descent have traditionally been. It therefore draws upon the whole of human experience for ideas and techniques that remain relevant to our own times and conditions.

Improvement demands that the reader select those techniques or methods that seem suited to his or her own circumstances, assemble them into a coherent, structured approach, and as time passes, modify and adjust that structure to accommodate change. It requires that one recognize both the persistency of human characteristics and the constancy of change in human affairs, and the fact that organisms (in this case, people and organizations) that fail to recognize and adapt to change in a timely manner do not prosper, and indeed may perish. If one accepts the assertion above - that development and growth as a manager is a part of a larger whole, development as a person - it follows that what one is as a whole person has enormous effect upon one's professional career. Those who successfully pursue a management career are threatened from within by their own ego and ambition and concupiscent appetites, and from without by critical scrutiny by peers, subordinates, superiors, stockholders, stakeholders, various forms of human vultures, and perhaps the courts of public opinion. Those who rise to high places in society have been judged, and continue to be judged, on the basis of how well their character befits their professional status. With responsibility and power come not only the status and rewards, but also the burdens of responsibility and power. Some of the accumulated experience of mankind is contained within the well-known biblical comment (at *Luke 12:48*), which may be stated as "Unto whomsoever much is given, of him shall the more be asked, and unto whomsoever men have entrusted much, of him shall they demand the more." In the eyes of the world, the quality of the person must accord with the level of the office.

Some scholars of management hold that managers, particularly middle managers, may rightly be considered an exploited class, because their entire life is centered upon and sometimes consumed by their presumed management responsibilities. A truly satisfying life as a manager must bring - along with responsibilities and power and income - adequate opportunity and time for love, parenthood, family, hobbies and recreation, personal growth and development, service to society: in sum, for the "pursuit of happiness." The book devotes some space to the matter of self-management and life management and, in parallel, to the manager's responsibility to his subordinates, peers, and the human community in these matters.

DECISION MAKING AND MANAGEMENT

Management's Central Product

It is a truism that the duties and responsibilities of "managers" differ widely. Put simply, managers do not all do the same things. Nevertheless, there is a definable set of functions, common to all managers, which prominently includes getting and absorbing information and making, communicating, and carrying out decisions. If one could define "management" with a single word or phrase, "decision-making" would immediately come to mind. One definition of "management" is "judicious use of means to accomplish an end," a clause which implies also judicious selection of an end. The primary and central product of management must therefore be "judicious decisions," and the organization that produces better and more timely decisions must gain a competitive advantage. Nevertheless, researchers have found that organizations are often poor decision-makers.[2] This book proposes, contrary to some opinion, that improvement in decision-making throughout an organization is attainable through well-established and teachable practices, which are described. As a corollary, it argues that decision-making prowess is not a gift conferred by the management gods upon the select few, but is instead achieved by study, practice, adoption and use of sound methodology, and personal and organizational development.

The reasons for poor managerial decisions are many and varied, and some will be examined later, but one requires mention here: many managers have had little or no formal training in decision-making methodologies, and many organizations have no clearly defined, structured, and visibly decision-making process. Consequently, they cannot and do not emphasize decision-making in their management training programs. It is not unusual, in such organizations, that decisions emerge from a black box called "management" and are announced, if at all, upon their implementation. Since we do not know what occurs inside the "black box," this does not preclude the possibility that good decisions can emerge in this way. Those who make the decisions within the "Black Box" have presumably demonstrated the necessary decision making qualities. So, if this manner of decision-making can work, what's wrong with it? Let us count the ways.

Two Essentials: Structure and Visibility

Recall the earlier assertion that we are all decision makers, and that decision making is the primary function of management, and therefore that we are all managers, if only of our own lives and careers. As an occupation, management can offer a lifetime of challenge, personal growth, and service. It is the guiding hand at the helm of human affairs, and therefore important to all human activities. On the other hand, managerial success has been aptly and simply defined as "getting the right things done right." That definition does not violate Einstein's dictum that "Everything should be made as simple as possible, but not more so." It cuts through the enormous volume of management literature, that both informs and overwhelms the reader, to get to the essence of management. Strategic management has been aptly defined as deciding the right things to do, and operational management as getting them done right. I assert that both are more a matter of having a plan on "how to make decisions" than on the personal qualities of talented individual managers. Without a structured decision making method, the management of both human lives and human enterprises works in darkness, groping for understanding of both problem and answer, and abjuring the advantages of both visible method and critical examination of its processes and results. In organizations, "Black Box" decision-making at best fails to inspire confidence and at worst engenders suspicion and cynicism in the organization's stakeholders (stockholders, employees, suppliers, customers, their families, governments, the public at large).

It is, of course, necessary at times that managements proceed toward an important decision in private, and announce the decision only after it has been finalized. It is the habit and practice of producing significant decisions in this manner, and not divulging either the process or the factors which were considered, that is in question here. The "black box" practice runs counter to the value systems of democratic societies that are the milieu in which Western organizations operate. The insistence by the voting populations of democracies that their representatives reach decisions by an open, visible and, by implication, rational and trustworthy process provides sufficient evidence of the concerns aroused by the "Black Box" phenomenon.

The need for visibility is manifested in our legal system. The "Freedom of Information Act" and various other "Sunshine" laws are manifestations of the American citizenry's demand that we not be governed by processes or motives not disclosed to us. We do not love the "press" or its modern equivalents "the media" and media figures, and we sometimes view the "media" or particular figures in it as untrustworthy, arrogant, biased, driven by ideology and generally no damn good, but we have no intention whatever of abridging their right to be any or all of those things. Instead, the media are occasional targets for inquiry into their own decision making processes and they must subject themselves to the same discipline of visibility they impose on others. It is not our love or hate for the media that motivates our attitudes, but our understanding that its function of providing reliable information is essential to our own decision-making. We cannot rid government or society of rascals and incompetents or raise persons of high character and ability to high office without free, competent, and vigorous media. We cannot assure that the information media retain and prize those qualities unless we demand and maintain the same visibility into their processes and integrity. Both the media and their watchers are vital to our decision-making processes.

In democratic political systems, such as that of the United States, many important decisions are left in the hands of voters who must rely on their general knowledge rather than some education in decision making. With greater knowledge of decision making and visibility into the processes candidates employ, voters might approach the ballot box with a sharpened judgment of the relative merits of the candidates. Candidates might enhance their prospects by describing and stressing their decision-making process, instead of promising certain decisions. Bismarck's famous comment, to the effect that it is better not to witness the process of making laws and sausages, reflects his observation that both can be products of badly flawed processes, and his apparent conclusion that the processes were immutable and best not open to observation. If the latter was indeed Bismarck's conclusion, human events have proved it to be mistaken: visibility into the decision-making process can lead to improvements.

Government is not the only human enterprise which elicits wide concern. Shareholders (more than one-half of all American families), employees (nearly all of us), and ordinary citizens have a stake in the quality of management of virtually every organization, therefore in the quality of management's decisions, and therefore in the openness and quality of the organization's decision-making process. Stakeholder awareness that major decisions are reached through a rational process and open argumentation enhances stakeholder confidence. That confidence in turn provides management greater flexibility by minimizing repeated misinformed challenges to particular management decisions.

All organizations have something to learn from this: a **visible, rational, structured** decision-making methodology allows stakeholders to gauge the quality of managerial decisions, and hence the quality of management, and hence the influence on their own lives. Visibility - transparency, if you like - and rationality instill among stakeholders the confidence in the organization's management that it needs for the occasional decisions it must reach through a private process. Finally, a visible and structured process, customarily followed by top management, serves as an example and training tool for all the echelons below it. Structured decision-making, properly applied, should improve the quality and reduce the costs of organizational decision-making by providing a clear process. It is universally understood that **making anything requires a process**, and that a bad process ordinarily cannot produce a good product. One should therefore not expect a poor decision-making process to produce good, timely decisions. Nor, of course, should one expect a good process to overcome erroneous data or poor reasoning. We shall get to the latter problem later.

Apart from the probability that a structured, rational process will produce better results, the use of such a process offers other advantages. A structured process as described in the following chapters outlines both the steps to be followed in reaching a decision and the documentation necessary to record those steps. It provides a clear audit trail of those steps; it records how the decision was perceived, who were the participants and what was their role. It illuminates the matter of when, where, and under what circumstances the decision was made. The value of an audit trail probably correlates closely with the importance of the decision. For decisions which may later be challenged via litigation or public airing, an audit trail is essential to the defense of the decision. It is also the indispensable basis for explaining the decision to those affected by it. The structured approach also inspires confidence that the organization is guided by a rational and visible process: nothing according to management's whims, nothing emerging from private, offline meetings of a self-chosen few. The structured decision-making process becomes an expression of the enterprise's management philosophy, its commitment to rational behavior and its willingness to face criticism. The establishment of a structured approach and its incorporation into the organizational culture may therefore be a means of inspiring confidence in the enterprise's management, both within and outside the enterprise. "Due diligence" in making decisions is both a concept and a legal requirement for most organizations. Conceptually, the performance of due diligence implies that a matter has been thoroughly investigated, the relevant facts gathered and verified, the assumptions stated and challenged, and both the facts and assumptions thought through before a decision is reached. "Due diligence" therefore requires a structured, documented approach. The methods recommended in this paper, when properly executed, represent "due diligence" and provide proof of it.

Some further definition of the terms used above may be useful. "Visible" or "transparent" do not imply that management decisions be reached in an auditorium, with decision-makers on stage before an audience of all stakeholders. Decision making in the limelight is clearly both impracticable for most decision-making situations and an undesirable constraint upon the free flow of thought and argumentation. The term "rational" is used in its ordinary sense of being based on or agreeable to reason. The term "argumentation" refers to discussion and debate as a non-adversarial process of collaborative effective reasoning. The term "structured" refers to an established, published, and understandable process that can, when necessary, provide the basis for tracing the reasoning and argumentation from origin through outcome, and thus for understanding what considerations led to the final decision. "Structure" can produce better decisions and provide a means of holding managements and governments responsible.

Perhaps for the latter reason, some managers would argue that process is unimportant or less important than personality, that the quality of decisions is a direct function of the mental capacity and personality of the decision-maker. The argument is important: as I noted earlier, if it is accepted it implies that decision-making proficiency is a virtue bestowed on a select few, and therefore not retrospectively visible and not teachable. It thus justifies the enormous monetary rewards and/or the enormous power granted to the top management of some enterprises, and the enormous power accorded to some authoritarian or dictatorial government figures. It is, moreover, the essential basis of dictatorial authority, the assertion of a right to make decisions for others on the ground that their decision making competence is inferior. I do not denigrate the importance of the "decision-maker's" personal qualities: they are, after all, what we are seeking to understand and enhance. The qualities of prudence and good judgment are not equally distributed, but the process I outline later in this and the next chapter can enhance those qualities where they exist, possibly implant them where they do not, and provide the skeletal framework that encourages their use.

Moreover, the habitual use of a visible rational process avoids the dangers of the "Black Box" that allows decision making to operate entirely shrouded from outside observation and audit. Structure thus can provide a constraint on arbitrary exercise of power.

Better Than A Black Box?

Let us here outline a decision-making system that would have a higher probability (than the "Black Box" approach) of both producing better decisions and inspiring greater confidence in those who might be affected by them. First, let's make some decisions about the required or desired characteristics of a decision making process, accepting some repetition of earlier observations. The process should be "structured" because it must be describable, teachable, and rational. The structured process should be easily grasped, and adaptable to decision making at all levels of importance, complexity, and organization. When employed by organizations, it should therefore be visible, published, and endorsed by senior management. It should be institutionalized, in the sense of being a permanent part of the organization's culture. It should be applicable to all disciplines and human activities. For significant decisions, it should provide a clear documented audit trail. It should create and maintain confidence and respect from management, employees, stockholders, stakeholders, and the general public.

The "structured, rational process of deciding" necessarily begins with the recognition of a matter requiring or benefitting from attention. How to do that, unless the daily flow of activities confronts us with the need to make a decision?

Decision making can be reactive or proactive. Reactive decision-making arises from events or circumstances that confront us with the necessity for deciding what to do, and leave no ambiguity regarding the necessity of deciding. Essentially, events or circumstances are in

charge: they come in a manner demanding some action. For organizations, the need comes in the form of correspondence, queries,
orders, purchases, sales, events: the things of daily business, often
first received by a mail room or its electronic equivalent and then
routed to the appropriate part of the organization. If the organization has been well designed, the routing function has recognized the
problem correctly and routed it appropriately. For individuals, the
need for reactive decisions arises from events and circumstances of
daily life.

In contrast, proactive decision-making has a "make it happen"
nature. The occasions for these decisions do not arise in the course
of daily events: organizations and individuals must seek them out
by constant and conscious alertness, or find them in the larger reality that underlies the surface of events. Proactive decisions address
the transition from the present to the future, seeking to anticipate
or cause potential events or circumstances, to identify future problems and opportunities, and to identify and rank the options to be
implemented if and when the occasion arises. Proactive decision-
making also identifies frequently recurring situations or events as
the basis for establishing broad policy covering an array of subordinate decisions. Proactive decision-making in organizations is the
essential basis for strategic planning and policy, for determining the
organization's mission and purpose as they exist and as its managers conclude they should become, and for determining *who decides
what* in the organization. It is also the essential basis for generating
ideas, the life blood of progress and adaptation to change. Because
the occasions for these decisions do not arise and confront us, they
must be sought out if we are to avoid the unrecognized problem
or opportunity, the path not perceived and therefore not taken.
The "situation audit" or its military/government counterpart, the
"Estimate of the Situation," provides the structured methodology

for identifying matters that pose the need or provide the opportunity for consequential change, and thus consequential decision-making. Both are discussed later.

In our personal lives, the category of proactive decision-making includes the decisions each of us ought to make, but often don't because it has not occurred to us that we need to establish life plans and set personal goals and standards. That decision, consciously made and carried out, defines and shapes one's character and persona, because it requires us to decide, as an organization must, our mission and purpose, our objectives and means: what we are and what we wish to become; what we want and what we are willing to do to get what we want, and what we will not do to get what we want. If that has been done, many other decisions, including the seemingly trivial, have already been made in principle and become much easier when the occasion to make them arises. For example, the ordinary problem of purchasing clothes is decided in principle in the words of the Greek philosopher Epictetus, who allegedly wrote "Know, first, who you are; and then adorn yourself accordingly." Matters of perhaps much greater significance are decided in principle, in advance, on the basis of our conception of who and what we are, and what we wish to become. This process must, of course, be repeated at various stages of life: it is vital to the process of renewal and adaptation as life and circumstances change.

I return now to the decision-making process. The word "problem" has a special meaning in its decision making context. A "problem" is a matter or circumstance that requires or may benefit from a decision. To solve a problem, one must first be able to state it explicitly. This counsel - "to define the problem" or "to define and limit the problem" - has become almost a cliché among consultants and operations research team members who have wide experience in being called in to solve problems for a wide variety of endeavors.

They have found that managements have sometimes, perhaps frequently, called upon them to address "problems" that have been poorly defined or incorrectly identified. Much time must then be spent on redefining the problem and getting management's agreement with the problem statement.

In some organizational cultures, the word "problem" is abhorred as reflecting adversely upon the organization. For those overwhelmed by such qualms, "Houston, we have a problem" would not be an admissible statement. Alternative words, such as "opportunity" or "purpose," may be more palatable for some managements. I do not recommend the use of "objective" in a problem statement, because it may foster confusion between the matter to be addressed and desired solution. The word "resolution" is used in contemporary argumentation literature to refer to a simple declarative sentence which describes the issue or matter being addressed, but it too is inadmissable in the decision making context because it may be confused with the desired outcome of the decision making process. A military staff study process, developed and refined over a period of centuries, begins with the requirement to **define and limit the problem,** employing a sentence beginning with an infinitive. I regard the word "problem," properly understood as a simple declarative or imperative sentence identifying the matter to be addressed, as suitable and non-pejorative, and use it hereafter. The use of the infinitive beginning allows a number of approaches, such as to determine, to estimate, to examine, to illuminate, to explore. In all cases, the infinitive beginning requires that a decision be made.

The problem statement shapes the nature of the process to solve it, and influences the outcome. Defining and limiting the problem requires, among other things, establishing limits upon the scope of the inquiry and the objective or objectives to be attained: if one limits the problem, one limits the potential measures to resolve it. The desired objective tends to intrude, insidiously or openly, at times necessarily, into the drafting of the problem statement. Objectives are more appropriately addressed under "Factors Bearing On the Problem," discussed below. We should note here that specifying the objective according to some "measure of effectiveness" or "payoff measure" is considered to be one of the most difficult problems in decision-making. Although the reasons for this are multiple and complex, they lie principally in the fact that every individual and every organization holds views and beliefs which lead them to value results according to some subjective criteria, often called "utility measure." In investing, for example, some investors might seek maximum monetary return, others would wish to avoid certain industries whose products might adversely affect the environment. In organizations, the roles of individuals and departments contending for primacy or high place or simply confining their thinking to their departmental role and interests influence the establishment of utility measures, often to the detriment of the objectives of the organization as a whole. The conflicts must be reconciled in some way, either by accepting multiple objectives according to some system of ranking or granting a single objective prime status over all others.

The corollary to establishing the objectives that are to be attained is identifying consequences that are to be absolutely avoided or held to a very low probability. This consideration ordinarily arises after a one sentence problem statement has been finalized. It identifies some factor or factors that may influence the range of possible outcomes. For example, one may place limits on cost and risks of various kinds. It is therefore feasible, and often desirable after having stated the problem, to design and describe a decision in conceptual terms by placing boundaries upon its desired and undesired consequences: that is, by describing what it must have a high probability of accomplishing, and what it must have a high probability of avoiding. In effect, this produces a functional specification for the decision, identifying some of the factors that bound the range of possible options.

It is clear, then, that one ordinarily cannot leap directly from the problem statement to solutions. In addition to identifying the constraints and desired characteristics of the solution, it is necessary to gather facts and make assumptions when facts are not available. But, the facts and assumptions must be relevant to the problem, and we must therefore identify the considerations that affect the problem. This requires that we "dissect" the problem, separate the various factors that affect it, analyze the influence of each, and then combine those analyses to assess their combined and cumulative effect. Because decision making involves future events and actions, almost all decision making situations require that we make assumptions. We often, perhaps usually, make these assumptions implicitly or tacitly: that is, without specifically identifying them, even to ourselves, and considering their reasonableness. An important aspect of decision-making therefore lies in making our assumptions explicit, and rigorously examining them for validity.

The preceding discussion leads to a general principle:

Decision making with respect to complex problems usually requires identifying the factors that influence the matter, analyzing each of them separately, and bringing together the results of the separate analyses.

This method has often been called by the obvious term: **factor analysis.** An understanding of each factor is gained, decisions are made with respect to each of the factors examined, and those decisions are drawn together to produce a **synthesis,** in the form of a broad decision that attempts to resolve conflicts or difficulties involved in addressing the various factors separately. The method is perhaps the most widely used in all formal decision making, because life rarely produces decision making situations that do not require resolution of competing or conflicting objectives.

Having produced such a synthesis, one is positioned to identify measures to address the problem. "Courses of action (COA's)," or "options," or "alternatives" are all terms often used to refer to measures one might take to resolve or improve any particular situation or matter. Properly understood, all are acceptable. However, "alternative" is often taken to mean the choice between two or more things of which only one may be chosen. The term "courses of action" has the virtue of implying that more than one choice may be made, and the fault of implying the inadmissability of doing nothing. I prefer the term "option" or "options" as more broadly encompassing all of the possible choices that may be made, and use it hereafter in that sense. An "option" is any "course of action" or "alternative" that may be selected. The options available always include the so-called "null option"; that is, the conscious decision to do nothing, or to do nothing at the present time. Conversely, selection of more than one option - a combination of measures - may represent a better decision than the selection of any single one.

The final phase of the decision making-process is identifying and assessing the set of options open to us and selecting an option or set of options calculated to maximize the foreseeable desired consequences and minimize the foreseeable undesired consequences. On reflection, it will seem obvious to the reader that this is the way decisions ought to be made. It is important, however, to distinguish between the desired nature of the process and characteristic human behavior in it. Clearly, for most decisions one cannot identify all the possible options. One cannot, for example, compare a prospective marriage partner with all the other potential marriage partners in the world, because we do not have the opportunity to meet all the others. Partly for that reason, most of us are what Herbert Simon has called "satisficers" rather than "optimizers" or "maximizers." "Satisficers" ordinarily devote no more time to identifying the available options and analyzing their desired and undesired consequences than is necessary to identify an option that is acceptable but not necessarily the best that might be chosen. In effect, this is an economic choice, a common sense method of balancing the amount of effort devoted to making the decision with the importance of the decision. Decision making has costs which may be in money, time, energy, stress, strife, opportunity (what must be forsaken if a particular decision is taken), or other measures. It is therefore entirely reasonable to balance the cost of decision making with the importance of the decision. The "satisficer" approach may therefore be appropriate in deciding many ordinary matters, but in halting the analysis at the first acceptable option it may be costly for matters of greater significance. For major decisions, most of us are more deliberate but not necessarily better organized or less inclined to be "satisficers." If we wish to improve our decision-making capabilities, or our ability to negotiate with a "maximizer" or "optimizer." we must be conscious of our "satisficer" characteristic. Simon and his associates also noted that rationality has limits, that humans have preferences for some "payoff measures" over others, and therefore that the term "bounded rationality" or "limited rationality" better fits the process ordinarily employed.[3]

In order to select the option or option set that best balances the foreseeable desired and undesired consequences of major decisions, it is

necessary to identify ALL the options that are re-alistically (not just possibly) open to us and ALL their desired and undesired consequences, and employ some weighting system to evaluate those consequences.

This may seem to impose a ponderous requirement, but it need not. It is often useful, even for less important decisions, to quickly define the problem, identify the available options, assess their fore-seeable desired and undesired consequences and the possibility of unforeseen consequences (what could go wrong?), and decide ac-cordingly. This approach can serve in one-on-one or group con-versations to keep the participants on topic. For most decisions, this can be accomplished in brief ordinary conversation. Making ordinary decisions in this way can also habituate the organization's personnel to the process, produce quicker and better decisions at all levels, and enhance both decision-making competence and con-fidence in what I will term "organizational rationality" at all levels. The general methodology for this process is well established. It recognizes that the term "rational" has a cultural context, that what seems "rational" to one decision-maker may appear to be "irratio-nal" to another, and that the emotions are also involved in decision making. The use of "measures of effectiveness" and/or "payoff func-tions" in selecting options allows for those differences. The terms "bounded rationality" model, "rational model," synoptic (i.e., whole or comprehensive) model" are among those used to refer to variants of the process suggested here.

The *Law of Unforeseen Consequences* has emerged as a result of human experience with decisions that produced conse-quences that were both unforeseen and undesired. Its parallel is the often noted phenomenon that hindsight is clearer than foresight. It is a useful reminder that we must consider the possibility that a particular decision may set in motion a chain of events or an action-reaction cycle whose outcome we cannot confidently foresee. "What could go wrong?" analysis is therefore an important aspect of decision-making. It is said that an Irishman named Houlihan discovered that if something could go wrong, it would, and that his discovery now is well known as Murphy's Law.

FINAL STEPS

We may now summarize the essentials of the decision making process, as it ought to be.

- **Define and limit the problem.**
- **Identify the objectives to be attained, and the consequences to be avoided.**
- **State the important assumptions explicitly.**
- **If appropriate or necessary, address each factor bearing on the problem separately, then draw the analyses together.**
- **Identify the options available to solve the problem.**
- **Assess the probable desired and undesired consequences of each option.**
- **Compare and contrast the consequences of the options.**
- **Select the option or options providing the best balance of desired and undesired consequences, according to the assumptions made and the objectives sought.**

This basic methodology, suitably adjusted for the complexity and importance of the decision being addressed and the costs of making it, can be applied to the entire range of human decisions. It provides a structured approach that imposes discipline and forces us to examine and validate our understanding of the problem, the boundaries to its solution, our assumptions, our facts, our reasoning, and our conclusions. It provides the essential "transparency" or "visibility" for important decisions by leaving, when appropriate, a traceable paper trail. It fulfills the requirement for "due diligence." It provides a paradigm for lower elements of the organization to adopt. It stimulates creativity by forcing us to cast our net widely in both defining the problem and seeking options to solve the problem as we have defined it. It does not - in fact it cannot and should not - prevent or prohibit the use of intuition (rightly understood as judgment) or personal preference (utility measures) in selecting options, but it does make us recognize the role of those factors in the decision.

I have earlier observed that the term "decision-maker" may apply to both individuals and groups. An organization may be perceived as a decision-making mechanism, in which decision-making is distributed according to senior management's perception of the differing characteristics and importance of the decisions to be made. The designers of the mechanism must themselves decide what decisions are made at what level in organizations, where and how and by whom they are to be made, when they must be made, what enters into their consideration, and what records must be kept. A prudent senior management will not delegate to subordinate units decisions which affect the entire organization or subject it to high risk. On the other hand, it must draw upon the decision-making capabilities of subordinate organizations and individuals, and it must delegate most decision-making to those subordinate units, simply because they are at the point where the needs for most decisions arise and the required relevant information is most readily available. This matter - determining "who decides what?" - is the essence of the organizing problem and thus one of the most important decision-making responsibilities of senior management, because that decision must precede all other decisions.

DON'T FORGET WILHELMINA

We must not leave this chapter without addressing the plight of the infant Wilhelmina. Did the parents make the right decision in naming her after the rich but eccentric great-aunty, both out of affection and with the hope that doing so would assure her a rich inheritance? Would it not have been better to provide her a more widely popular or "success image" name, anticipating that she must make her own way in life, regardless of Aunt Wilhelmina's bounty or lack thereof? Shakespeare asked, "what's in a name?" Does the name Wilhelmina compromise her prospects of success in her own endeavors? Each reader will, of course, see the answer to these questions from his or her own utility measure. Consider, however, one final point not previously introduced in our discussion: what are the probable consequences of _not_ naming her Wilhelmina? And, place in memory the fact that this is a general question that should be raised, along with those previously outlined, in any decision-making situation. Meanwhile, do not worry: we shall meet Wilhelmina again.

Chapter 2

Using the Process

USES AND MISUSES

The Range of Applicability

The discussion in the preceding chapter has outlined the syntax - the sequence of steps in a "connected and orderly system"- for both formal (written and staffed) and informal decision-making: Problem$\Rightarrow$ Factors Bearing on the Problem$\Rightarrow$Assumptions$\Rightarrow$Facts and Discussion$\Rightarrow$Conclusions$\Rightarrow$Decision or Action (usually, when prepared by a staff, "Action Recommended"). As we shall see later, the methodology is not immune to error or misuse, but it is a very useful decision-making tool. In addition to its evident rationality, the methodology has credentials based on long usage. It is essentially that of the comprehensive military staff study and executive branch of the Federal Government decision paper. The logical flow of papers prepared for high level government decisions was drawn from Army staff practice and set in place by Eisenhower's White House Chief of Staff Walter B. Smith, who had also been Eisenhower's Chief of Staff in his World War II role as Supreme Commander Allied Forces Europe. Successive national administrations have changed the names and somewhat altered the formats, and some no doubt have reached decisions via the "Black Box" approach, but the sequence outlined here has largely endured as a model. Because it provides the essential syntax and structure for orderly decision-making, approaches very similar to it are widely used in a variety of decision-making situations and locales. It has versatility and wide applicability. For important decisions, it may be enlarged to cover every factor in depth, written, circulated in draft and extensively "staffed," subjected to peer review, critiqued, and rewritten. In less formal decision-making situations, it can be employed in checklist fashion to assure that an orderly, structured process has been conducted and all the important considerations identified and assessed. The syntax can provide a locus, a central thread , for discussion in any "where are we, whither are we tending, what shall we do?" situation. The discussion, oral or written, can begin with the problem statement and work through the factors, assumptions, and options to a conclusion and recommendations. In typical one-on-one and small meetings conducted in a conversational mode, rough presentation aids or a whiteboard may suffice to record and emphasize the major points. A written statement of the problem keeps the dialogue focused. The informal atmosphere that is valuable in discussions of this nature can be maintained within the structured decision-making process. If a written record is useful or required, the substance of the discussion, including all the major considerations, can be recorded in a memorandum for the record, following substantially the formats outlined below. In sum, then, the process provides the opportunity and structure for rational consideration and decision-making, and it can be adopted by both organizations and individuals as their standard methodology for decision-making. On the other hand, it cannot guarantee against deliberate misuse, incorrect information, selective use of information, faulty reasoning, bias, and other pitfalls. We shall address some of these misuses later.

The Formal, Six-part, Study Format

For major decisions, the process is incorporated into the formal, comprehensive, six-part decision-making study format. The FACTS AND DISCUSSION portion provides the main body of the study, including identification and consideration of the options available, and comparisons to aid in selecting a single option or a combination of options that appear to be best suited to the problem. The CONCLUSION part includes the selected options and summarizes the reasoning supporting their selection. Most of the remainder of this chapter addresses the process of fact gathering, reasoning, and dialogue that is encapsulated in this study format. The major headings are:

PROBLEM (or, if one prefers, PURPOSE or MISSION)

FACTORS BEARING ON THE PROBLEM

ASSUMPTIONS

FACTS AND DISCUSSION

CONCLUSION

RECOMMENDATIONS (or ACTION RECOMMENDED)

The Three Part Format

The format for the less complex decisions is ordinarily a condensed version of the six-part format outlined above. The three-part format provides the decision maker an adequate basis for a relatively routine matter, such as signing a response letter or authorizing a payment or purchase.

PROBLEM (or, if one prefers, PURPOSE or MISSION)

A single declarative sentence, ordinarily beginning with an infinitive, that conveys the intended outcome.

FACTS AND DISCUSSION

For most decisions, one or more paragraphs as necessary to state the essential facts and   assumptions and identify and evaluate the available options.

CONCLUSIONS AND RECOMMENDATIONS

One paragraph, possibly two. The recommendations state the action or actions proposed.

In all or any of its variants, the preceding syntax provides only a skeletal framework that must then be fleshed out. We turn now to some observations on that matter.

Defining and Limiting the Problem (or Purpose or Mission)

To reiterate earlier observations, it is   critically important to get the problem (or purpose or mission) right if we are to get the decision right. The use, or misuse, of the word "problem" can itself lead to misunderstanding. The statement should not be a description of symptoms. Custom and long usage require a single sentence beginning with an infinitive, allowing for elaboration in the later discussion. It should identify what the paper, or the activity that produces it, is to accomplish. Getting the problem right requires not only overcoming the difficulties of natural language, but also deciding exactly what it is that we are trying to decide. To test this proposition, think of any decision problem you may have and write a description of it. Do you believe that your first attempt correctly defines and limits the problem? Have you avoided the common errors in such statements? Suppose, for example, young Wilhelmina, having reached the early stage of adult life and entered the work force, has decided that her hopes for financial independence lie in going into business for herself. She lacks the necessary capital, and writes the following statement of her problem.

PROBLEM

1. To borrow $50,000 from Great-Aunt Wilhelmina to go into business.

Here young Wilhelmina has committed two common errors. The first one: failing to distinguish between objectives and means. Going into business is, in this instance, an objective, although it may also be considered as a means, as discussed below. Borrowing $50,000 is a means of obtaining capital to go into business. The second error: selecting, without weighing it against other options, the option of borrowing it from great-aunt Wilhelmina. That is one of several potential means of obtaining $50,000, and is also a solution statement rather than a problem statement. By prematurely selecting this option, Wilhelmina has excluded the potential of borrowing the money from a bank, a group of friends, or other sources. Moreover, if young Wilhelmina has followed an orderly, structured process of decision-making, she will have selected going into business for herself as the preferred option from a number of possible options to achieve some larger goal in life. If she has not completed or even attempted that process, her problem is neither going into business for herself nor borrowing $50,000 from Great-Aunt Wilhelmina to do so: it is determining what she wishes to do with the foreseeable part of her life, and what options appear best suited to the attainment of her current objectives. She has also failed to take into account the possibility of an undesired or unanticipated consequence in going first to Great-Aunt Wilhelmina. Aunty Wilhelmina may be very loving as well as very rich and slightly dotty, but not crazy enough to part with fifty thousand dollars without some sharp questioning of niece Wilhelmina's motives for going into business, her due diligence in preparing to do so, the quality of her business plan, and her prospects for payment of the loan. If the answers to these questions prove inadequate, Aunt Wilhelmina is likely not only to refuse the loan but also to be more guarded in her future relationship with her namesake. On the other hand, if niece Wilhelmina has produced a sound business plan, it would include the specifics of the business she proposes to enter, her consideration of how much capital is needed and identification of the options for obtaining it. In that case Great-Aunt Wilhelmina may very well ask why the option of obtaining it from her, rather than from a bank or other financing institution, has been selected.

This little story has its direct counterpart in the world of affairs. Suppose, for example, a manufacturing company becomes aware that some of its products are not selling well, and its management accordingly creates an internal multi-disciplinary group to address the matter. The problem assigned to the group should not read "some of our products are selling poorly." That statement describes a symptom. A better problem statement, one that does define and limit the problem, might read "To identify products that are not selling satisfactorily, to learn why, and to recommend remedial measures." If management desired a broader examination, the problem statement might read "To identify the optimum product mix for maximum profitability during the period two to seven years ahead," recognizing the time required to alter the product mix.

It is very easy to believe that we, as managers of our own personal realm, or the managers of any human enterprise, understand the problem to be addressed. Why would we have become interested in it if we did not understand it? The answer is perhaps most starkly provided by experience. Groups or individuals asked to address a problem have often found it necessary to recast the problem statement several times in the course of their early work, and ultimately to obtain management's concurrence in a substantially revised version. One of innumerable examples is provided by health care giant Kaiser Permanente's effort to develop a long-range growth plan. Kaiser Permanente's management stated the task as "to attract more patients and cut costs." That statement - to develop a plan "to attract more patients and cut costs" - describes the problem as Kaiser's management perceived it, and that formulation was accompanied by a management view of how those aims might best be achieved. Kaiser was at that time the largest health management organization in the U. S., and was widely regarded as perhaps the best managed. Obviously, a long-term growth plan is very important, and in initiating it Kaiser management "thought it might have to replace many . . . {medical offices and hospitals} with expensive next-generation buildings." It hired a design firm, Ideo, to help. "Kaiser execs didn't know it then, but they were about to go on a fascinating journey of self-discovery." Ideo social scientists, designers, architects and engineers teamed up with Kaiser's medical personnel, some times playing the role of patients themselves. They concluded that an overhaul of the total patient experience, rather than construction of numerous new facilities, was needed.[1] As one Kaiser manager put it, "Ideo showed us that we are designing human experience, not buildings. Its recommendations did not require big capital expenditures." (We should note that the Ideo-Kaiser team conducted a "Situation Audit," evidently without using that term to describe it.)

The Kaiser-Ideo experience is usual. Similar accounts are common in the literature of several disciplines: for example, management, operations research, psychology, and decision-making. This implies that senior managements are sensitive to important issues, but not very good at rigorously defining the issues and determining what to do about them. The reasons why that should be the case are readily apparent. Senior management is engaged in the daily press of business, it is dependent upon information and recommendations flowing upward from within the organization or from outside the organization, and it lacks time to examine in depth the realities underlying this daily flow. It has been said that an expert is someone who knows more and more about less and less. It could, with equal appropriateness, be said that a professional senior manager is someone who knows less and less about more and more, and is increasingly dependent upon information provided by more specialized subordinates as he or she rises in position and responsibility. Senior management may be aware of problems for some time, but immediate and urgent matters command attention. The less immediate and more consequential for the long term may continue until senior management recognizes that it must address them, often through a task group staffed from various departments and disciplines within the organization. If the concern is sufficiently great, as in the Kaiser Permanente case, a comprehensive examination of the organization's situation and prospects may be required.

The daily business of living involves similar difficulties in describing the problem to be addressed. Let's take an example from ordinary life. You own and use an automobile that has earned your affection and a correspondingly affectionate name ("Exploder," perhaps) but is nearing the end, date uncertain, of its useful life. Your initial view is, correctly, that: 1) you must replace that automobile in the foreseeable future; 2) the cost of doing so is an important consideration in the family financial picture. Your initial problem statement might then be "To replace the Exploder," and you are immediately aware that this objective requires nothing more than a trip to the dealer. That, however, is the "satisficer" approach. On reflection, you recognize that what must be replaced, or added to, or subtracted from, is the car's "utility": that is, what it has been doing for you. The "state of nature" has changed since you bought the car. As you begin addressing the problem statement, you recognize some questions suggested by Kipling's little verse from *The Elephant's Child:*

I keep six honest serving men

(They taught me all I knew)

Their names are What and Why and When

And How and Where and Who.

Or, you may choose the easily remembered formulation: Who, What, When, Where, Why, and How. Who will drive: middle-aged spouse, college senior daughter, sixteen year old son? Why?: to commute to work, to pull a boat trailer, to take long trips? When?: at night, in wintry weather, in mountainous terrain, or in desert conditions? Where?: from suburban home to city work place? What?: at highway speeds, or in stop-and-go congestion? When is the most advantageous time to buy? Other factors - such as initial cost, depreciation, financing and monthly payments versus other demands on income, maintainability, fuel consumption and fuel cost, and safety - must be addressed, but this discussion suffices to show that the initial draft problem statement for a major household expenditure is not unlike that for a major business investment or expenditure. Both should be understood as an entry point, with the expectation that greater understanding and reflection will result in changes in one's perception of the problem.

Factors Bearing on the Problem

I have recommended the method of "factor analysis," which requires us to break down our problem into an appropriate number of pieces, to analyze and evaluate those pieces, and then to bring the results of each separate analysis and evaluation into a whole. Influential factors (considerations) are of two kinds: those unique to the particular problem, and those common to all, or nearly all, problems. The specific factors relevant to a particular problem are, of course, identifiable only by addressing that problem, and hence outside the scope of discussion here. It is useful, however, to identify some classes that are widely recurring and relevant. For example, every decision making situation has some limits, which we may classify as constraints upon the decision options, and others as criteria that must be met. The constraints ordinarily include monetary cost; financing; opportunity cost; time; availability or obtainability of necessary personnel and equipment, and skills; organizational culture; risk of failure, and willingness to commit. Criteria ordinarily include one or more "payoff functions": probability of profit, growth, or other desired form of gain; assurance against loss; enhancement of capabilities and reputation; assured entry into a new area of activity. In matters where significant decisions are envisioned by a major organization, some of the common factors emerge from the fact that major changes will be perceived as advantageous by some "stakeholders," adverse by others. The final decision must take "stakeholder" interests into account, requiring that those interests be identified, analyzed, and evaluated as factors. "Stakeholders" include all persons and organizations whose interests might be affected by the decision: for example, stockholders, customers or clients, employees, suppliers, creditors and debtors, competitors, distributors and retailers of the organization's products or services, advocacy ("cause") organizations, environmentalists, governments, and perhaps others. In many important decision-making situations, there also exists a vaguely perceived, vaguely defined, often dormant but always potentially influential phenomenon known as "the public interest." Philosophers have long observed that "man seeks the good," and a later chapter addresses that historical fact. Here let it suffice that, in practical terms, the term "public interest" is substituted for "the good." Decisions that are widely perceived by the media and/or the public as adverse to the public interest encounter opposition and may be difficult or impossible to implement. The "good," or the "public interest," is always a potential stakeholder, and correspondingly should always be considered.

Having identified the factors that influence the matter, one must then obtain relevant facts, a matter of sufficient importance and difficulty to merit its own examination later. In the absence of facts, we must make some assumptions, and we proceed to that requirement.

More on the Need for Assumptions

The biblical concept that "we know in part, and we prophesy in part" explains the need for assumptions in many decision-making cases. Assumptions bridge the gap between what we know or can confidently predict, and what is either unknown at decision time or is unknowable, such as the course of future events. Much of what we do or plan to do requires assumptions, and because they are commonplace we often make them implicitly rather than explicitly. Take the simple case of daily routine. We plan to go to work tomorrow morning, and we plan to be on time. We assume implicitly, then, that our place of work will be intact and open, that our automobile will start and run satisfactorily or that public transportation will perform as usual, that our route to work or public transportation will allow the normal time in transit, that we shall be well and fit for the day's work, and so on. Given the prevailing "state of nature," all of these are perfectly reasonable. They amount to a more general assumption that the future will be like the present and past. We do not have to make them explicit, and doing so would represent a substantial waste of effort. But, there are decision-making situations that demand explicit assumptions. Here are two examples from an electric power company's 2004 filing with the United States Securities and Exchange Commission:

The power industry continues to transform into a more competitive market.

As the supply-demand picture improves, we expect to see spark spreads [profit margins on sales] improve and capital markets regain their interest in helping to repower {sic} America with clean, highly efficient energy technologies.[2]

These "forward-looking" statements by the Calpine Corporation are assumptions. The first explicitly assumes that a perceived contemporary trend will continue, and implicitly assumes that a more competitive market will be to the company's advantage. The second assumes three eventualities: the supply-demand "picture" will improve (demand will increase more rapidly than supply), the company's profit margins will therefore improve, and the company will therefore be able to secure financing for new projects and the recycling of existing debt. These assumptions, predicting a changed "state of nature," provided the essential basis for the company's strategic plan. Similar "forward-looking" statements - assumptions with respect to future conditions - appear in virtually every organizational plan and every political campaign. The fact that they are explicit and published provides all stakeholders opportunity and incentive for "what could go wrong?" analysis, but also demands critical search for implicit assumptions. Identifying the need for assumptions, and expressing them explicitly and precisely, requires considerable diligence and intellectual honesty on the part of those formulating them. Incidentally, the Calpine Corporation's assumptions proved to be wildly optimistic: Calpine dismissed its founder and other top executives in December 2005, and filed for Chapter 11 bankruptcy.[3] It has since emerged from bankruptcy.

This example is one of an innumerable many that exemplify the need for critical review and "what could go wrong?" analysis, not only of assumptions but also of purported facts. Consider the potential effect, in the above case, of questioning whether any, to say nothing of all, of the above "forward looking" judgments would prove to be correct. Consider how those judgments might have changed if Calpine's management had recognized and confronted the corollary to the above assumptions: i.e., that for Calpine to survive and prosper, the competitive situation would have to change in its favor, AND overall demand for electric power would have to increase, AND profit spreads would have to improve accordingly, AND lenders would then provide financing for new projects and recycling of existing debt. We shall later introduce the concept of probability to considerations of this nature. Here let it be stated that if the probability of each of the four assumptions were 75%, or .75, the odds would be strongly against the predicted favorable outcome.

The Analysis Phase

Having developed an understanding of the "problem" and re-defined it, and having identified the factors bearing on it and the assumptions which must be explicitly stated, we are ready for the final step: determining what to do, and how to do it. This will require collecting and assessing information, reasoning, constructive argumentation (dialogue), obtaining additional facts and viewpoints, identifying and assessing and comparing options, and finally emerging with confident conclusions and recommendations. Although the conclusions should, and ordinarily do, follow logically from this effort under the "FACTS AND DISCUSSION" rubric, both the conclusions and the resultant recommendations are nevertheless judgment calls. This is the point at which one's biases, preferences, emotional attachments, and experience in life determine one's view of the *payoff function*, the risks involved, the probability of success, the consideration of what could go wrong, and the weight that should be accorded to the each of the various factors that have been identified and examined. These activities are addressed in the following chapters.

Chapter 3

Deciding What to Decide

GETTING IN THE MODE

The Fabled Decision Maker: Concept and Reality

The term-of-convenience "Decision-Maker" is commonly used to speak or write of the decision-making role in an abstract way: that is, without reference to or association with any particular person, group, or instance. The concept is important to us for both our own decision-making and for judging the decision-making qualities of those who may make decisions in our behalf: elected officials, employers, employees, associates, suppliers, families, friends. It allows one to address the qualities desired in the decision-maker in the abstract or theoretical sense, and to judge one's own and others' performance against some paradigm. In the concrete sense, one could usefully paraphrase Pogo's famous "we have met the enemy, and they is us" to "we have met the Decision Maker, and they is us." To reiterate earlier comments, the "decision maker" may be a single individual, two individuals with similar or dissimilar backgrounds, a group whose members represent a single discipline or a number of disciplines, a committee, a corporate board of directors, a city or county commission, a jury, the head of a state, the U. S. Supreme

Court, the Congress, the individual voter, the electorate, and so on. It is therefore useful to think of the decision maker in terms of "decision-making units," which may have many forms and compositions, their commonality lying in the decision-making function.[1] We perceive decision-making units as comprised of individual humans who may make final decisions on their own or be participants in a group decision making unit. Our first concern is therefore with means to improve the performance of the individual human as decision maker.

A Useful First Step

Humans do not have the exclusive charter to think and decide. One can readily observe and recall the thinking and acting of trained domesticated animals. Wild animals clearly absorb information, appraise it mentally, react to it emotionally, make decisions, and take actions (e. g., run or fight, attack or retreat) on the basis of their own mental and emotional processes. If one defines the decision making process as identifying a matter to be decided, obtaining the necessary information to decide it, and acting accordingly, one can argue that some plants make decisions. Flesh-eating plants determine that some object has contacted them, close on that object, determine if it is edible, and either reject it or absorb it. It is also true that machines make and execute decisions, in accordance with human design and programming. The microprocessor springs instantly to mind, making innumerable decisions in virtually every spectrum of human activity. In historical terms, this is a phenomenon of the computer era, in which enormous gains in human productivity have been made through decision-making by computers. This is a continuation of a long historical process: machines that sense conditions and take action with respect to them have been in use for centuries. The mechanical governor to control the speed of the steam engine dates from the early period of the Industrial Revolution, and its underlying principle has since found many other uses. The thermostat that senses the temperature in your home, and turns the heat or air conditioning unit on or off is a more recent example. The automobile is only one example of contemporary applications of the microprocessor to control machine and industrial processes, and much research is directed toward finding new decision-making applications for the microprocessor. The decision-making machine is, then, our creation. Nevertheless, we may have something to learn from it.

We can learn, from the behavior of the machine, a second characteristic useful for our own decision making behavior. Machine decision-making is an application of decision making under certainty or employing known or assumed probabilities. The process is structured. It is devoid of emotion, subjectivity, intuition, snap judgment. It does not brush aside incoming information that conflicts with its established convictions or its perceived "state of nature." It recognizes that organisms and organizations must adapt to changed conditions or improved understanding of existing conditions, or suffer adverse consequences. It is disciplined: it recognizes the need and moment to switch from an information gathering and monitoring mode to a decision-making mode. Examples: a search radar detects a target, identifies it, assigns a designator to it, and continues to track it while continuing its search for other possible targets; a computer program detects that an item in an inventory has dropped to or below the reorder point, and reorders it.

Although we are all at times decision makers, we are also not machines: we cannot totally set aside our emotions, convictions, our subjective preferences, our sexuality, our tendency for our attention to wander. We can, however, recognize that **we can have a decision-making mode**, to which we can switch when we sense the need for a decision, somewhat as the search radar "locks on" to a target it has detected and identified.

What Is the Decision-Maker Mode?

The **decision-making mode** is a conscious state of mind in which our critical faculties are alerted, our attention is focused on a particular matter. Our mental powers have locked onto that matter as a trained bird dog locks on, in intense quivering concentration, to the odor of his quarry. We are acutely and predominantly aware that we have become for a time, the fabled **decision-maker**. We have been alerted to the opportunity to get it right or to blunder. The trigger for this conscious switch to **decision-maker mode** must, like our watchful machines, be set mentally in advance: it is recognition that a **significant** decision-making situation has arisen, and that a serious approach to it is necessary. For ordinary, everyday decision making, it is of course, unnecessary to switch consciously to that mode. If the occasion for the important decision has been planned and scheduled in advance, the mode switch has been preset and should be **ON**. It is therefore particularly important to recognize the unscheduled and unplanned necessity for a significant decision, the "unanticipated or sudden decision-making occasion," and thus to avoid an offhand or other ill-considered reaction. In this reactive situation, events are in charge, in the sense that they confront us with the necessity "do something," and the consequent opportunity to do or say the wrong thing and repent later. To avoid that mistake, we must switch from the reactive mode to the consciously proactive. From somewhere in our brain, bells must ring, sirens go off in our minds, a message must emerge: "wait a bit, this situation requires a **Switch to Decision-Maker mode**." From that point, we lock onto the matter before us, and revert to the first qualification of the good decision-maker: the use of a decision-making process tailored to the occasion and the time available. The second essential quality of the good decision-maker is, then, the ability to recognize a serious decision-making situation and to bring to bear **The Decision-Maker Mode**.

The ability to recognize a serious decision making situation applies also to the proactive decision making mode, but the means of identifying the important decision making situations differ. We turn to the proactive decision-making process below.

THE PROACTIVE MODE

The Situation Audit and Its Uses

Reactive decision making occasions arise when the need for them confronts us. Proactive decision-making occasions arise from the decision-maker's search for matters requiring or benefitting from some action. This activity is important. Reactive decision-making addresses only the obvious. Problems, or opportunities, do not necessarily inform us of their presence or prospective appearance or magically land on our desk. They often lie in the shadows of circumstance and events, and the good decision maker must seek, identify, illuminate, and address them. How might one conduct that search? One well-proven method lies in the "Situation Audit."

The concept of the "situation audit" is succinctly captured in Abraham Lincoln's famous "House Divided Speech" before the Republican Convention at Springfield, Illinois, June 16, 1858: "If we could first know where we are, and whither we are tending, we could then better judge what to do, and how to do it." The situation audit is simply what its name implies: an examination of an organization's (or, an individual's) situation and prospects; where it is, and whither it is tending.

An organism (any living being) or an organization must adjust to changed circumstances ("states of nature") or fail in some major way, or perish. An annual situation audit, or one done more frequently if necessary, provides some assurance against failure to recognize an unsatisfactory existing or prospective situation in a timely manner. We can usually recognize an abrupt change in our surrounding circumstances, and thus recognize the need for a situation audit to address the recognized change. But, changes may lie and accumulate unseen below the surface of events: a cold or hot day is perceptible, a cold or hot season or year or extended period may not be. The situation audit serves as an early detection system. Consider, for example, a person's annual physical examination, or a woman's mammogram as an audit of the body's state of health, an annual "checkup." The same principle can well be more broadly applied to other aspects of human lives and careers and the fortunes of human organizations.

A situation audit for an organization may be as limited or as comprehensive as management sees fit. The "comprehensive" situation audit represents a major step in defining and limiting an organization's problems and opportunities. It is the essential basis for developing a long-term strategic plan, but it may also expose conditions that can be improved immediately or without a formal plan. Because it constitutes the basis for long-term planning, it should be conducted by those persons who must develop the plan and carry it forward. In practice, that means managers at all levels. A parallel effort by every member of the organization, to examine their own situations and prospects and develop their own self-development and career-development plan, should be encouraged. In this manner, the organizational development process reaches every element and individual in the organization, and offers individuals opportunity to develop their own career plans in light of their employer's plans.

For an individual, a situation audit might extend beyond career and employment prospects to include an assessment of the state and prospects of one's health, physical condition, appearance, education, marriage and family if appropriate, interpersonal relations, finances, career situation and prospects, overall life situation. The self-assessment should then provide the basis for an action plan.

An organizational situation audit provides a significant learning and training experience and a shared understanding of the organization's situation and prospects. It can be a "team building" experience. The senior managers directing the audit can learn much about the abilities of the subordinates by observing their performance of their own situation audit and their reporting of it via oral or written presentations, or both. The audit provides an opportunity for managers to coach their subordinates, and in turn to learn from them. It provides visibility into the contrast, if it exists, between what senior managers think is important and what their subordinates think is important, and opportunity to bring their respective perceptions into harmony. It provides managers and subordinates exposure to each other.

A comprehensive audit requires a considerable investment in management's time and efforts. A situation audit aimed at providing the basis for a complete organizational plan should be designed from an initiative provided by senior management, and the detailed design for the audit approved by senior management. If the organization has a planning staff, the staff has an obvious role in designing the situation audit and acting as a consultant to those actually conducting it. The document presented for management decision should integrate the results of these efforts into a comprehensive set of findings and recommendations for the entire organization.. Top management may accept, reject, or modify the findings and recommendations of the audit team.

In summary, the situation audit seeks comprehensive understanding of the organization's or individual's present situation, the external and internal influences that produced that situation, and the prospects for the future if no changes are made. The long-employed "estimate of the situation" and the "commander's estimate" are military versions of the "situation audit." The terms refer, of course, to both a study and thought process and to the document which records its methods and results.

Like any decision, the decision to launch a comprehensive study of an entire organization involves both desired and undesired consequences. The undesired consequences include both financial and opportunity costs, as the effort draws personnel and resources from other activities to conduct the study. Announcement that a comprehensive audit is to be undertaken creates expectation of change, which can in turn produce stakeholder concerns that changes will affect their interests adversely. It may stimulate employee fears that something is seriously wrong with the organization. Those conducting the audit may have unrealistic expectations that their recommendations will be uncritically accepted and implemented by management. Findings and views unevaluated by management may be leaked as the audit proceeds. Any and all of these developments may constrain the latitude of senior decision-makers in considering the recommendations produced by the audit.

There are ways to avert or minimize the undesirable consequences. An audit can be conducted within the existing organizational framework as an ongoing project and held at a low "noise level." A fairly comprehensive review can, with advance preparation and management guidance, be conducted at a management "retreat" at a location apart from that of the enterprise. But, it must also cover some minimal ground. I have found it useful, when examining organizations, to think of its minimal scope in terms of the nemonic "P's": purpose, plans, people (including employees, customers, shareholders, the public), products, productivity, processes, profitability, position in its market, prospects. Here are a few sample questions addressing an organizational audit. What is the present and prospective "state of nature" (set of circumstances external to the organization, including the existing and prospective market and economic conditions)? Do we have the right mission and purpose for the present and future, and have we defined our mission? Do we have the right people in the right organizational structure and geographic places to accomplish the right purposes? Do our products and/or services fit the existing and prospective market circumstances? How can we improve productivity by product and distribution changes? Are our production, distribution, and decision-making processes adequately defined and freed of excessive bureaucracy? In the context of the current and prospective future situations, what are our strengths, our weaknesses, our opportunities, and what threatens our endeavors? The latter questions, regarding strengths, weaknesses, opportunities, and threats are usefully remembered as the "SWOT Factors": Strengths, Weaknesses, Opportunities, Threats. The SWOT factors may be usefully applied to individuals (including oneself) as well as organizations.

These questions are representative only. A comprehensive guide may be found in a number of publications dealing with organizational strategy and planning.[2] The various guides are useful, particularly when the purpose is to provide a basis for a complete strategic plan.

When should an organization or an individual undertake a situation audit? Answer: 1) when an enterprise with no written and widely understood strategic plan has reached a point in its development at which it is no longer feasible to manage it "out of the boss's hat;" 2) when the existing plan has become outdated; 3) when a new management has been installed; 4) when a significant change in the external or internal circumstances under which the enterprise has operated has occurred or appears likely; 5) in anticipation of such a change; 6) when there is a perceived need to resolve competing ideas within the organization, regarding its future path; 7) when management identifies a need to intervene in and resolve rivalries and festering unresolved issues within the organization; 8) periodically, as insurance against complacency. An individual manager should assess her own situation at any time, and every time, she assumes new or additional duties and responsibilities or a major change in her situation occurs.

The situation audit should produce one or more options that are feasible, practicable, legal, moral, ethical, and reasonable. (I provide more on these criteria later.) The decision to be made is, then, to select the option or combination of options seen as best suited.

The audit can expose problems and opportunities, strengths and weaknesses, that can be immediately addressed, as well as others more deeply rooted and controversial, and therefore requiring a longer term effort. It provides a basis for shaping or reshaping an organization, perhaps requiring a new strategic plan. I have earlier noted that any decision advantages some and disadvantages others. There are, therefore, organizational winners and losers in any organization restructuring or change in strategic direction. Those who expect to lose can be expected to dissent. Others can dissent because they believe the recommendations are inappropriate. Dissents are necessary to good decision making because they provide the decision maker insight into both the reasons for not doing something recommended, and for doing something not recommended. Written dissents should be encouraged because they sharpen understanding of the issues that management must resolve, they sharpen the dissenters' thinking, and they may provide insight into the difficulties that might arise in carrying out the recommended actions. They also provide an audit trail. Management may wish to treat failure to dissent in writing as assent.

Management, having been handed a set of recommendations and issues, must now choose. It will have learned something, and ordinarily will have learned a great deal. Decision makers should have a good understanding, at this point, of "where we are and whither we are tending," but may not have reached a decision on "what to do." The situation audit may have starkly identified issues that provide a starting point for deliberation, for weighing the arguments of both advocates and dissenters, and for allowing a consensus to develop within the organization. If the recommendations propose high risk measures or major changes, a wise management will have provided for a period of time for itself and other stakeholders to absorb the report and recommendations, reflect upon them, and attain confidence on two issues: that the measures to be taken are the best options open, and that support for them within the organization is strong enough for them to be implemented effectively. That decision grows from deliberation, dialogue, the maturing and coalescing of thought to a consensus or conviction. Some of the measures that support both this process, as well as any significant decision-making effort, are outlined below and in the following chapters.

THE ABSORPTION MODE

Go. Talk. Listen. Look.

Of necessity, managers must spend a large part of their active work hours at their desks, which as their work station is the destination point for most of the flow of information and tasks. The mental portrait of reality produced at the desk may, however, differ substantially from the actuality. Periodically leaving one's desk, visiting facilities, talking and listening to people who do not often have opportunity to discuss their views, and generally soaking up grassroots information can produce a different and possibly more realistic perception of problems and opportunities, or the depth and extent of feeling with respect to identified issues. In his memoirs, former Secretary of State Dean Acheson noted that policy "bubbles up from below." Well and good, sufficiently true, but why wait for the bubble to reach the top or gamble that it will not be sidetracked in that journey? Organizations may be aptly thought of as communications systems, in which each little box on the organization chart is a "store-and-forward" or a "store-or-forward" node in a communication system. Managers cannot pass upward or laterally every piece of information they receive. Moreover, they may choose to store, at least for a time, information that they consider as reflecting adversely on them or likely to bring unwanted attention from their seniors. Important information may therefore reside at several layers below a particular manager's level. Although managers at intervening levels may not welcome visits and person-to-person discussions with their subordinates, and even threaten subordinates with reprisals, the practice of occasional impromptu "Go, talk, listen, look" visits may provide senior managers with a better understanding of reality. Much can be learned by impromptu meetings with a number of employees, in which the senior manager simply asks what, if anything, they would like to discuss, or any ideas they might wish to propose. It is important, of course, to assure that the originator of an accepted idea is appropriately recognized.

Peer Review and Criticism

The good decision maker seeks the advice and counsel of others, but is not prisoner to their views. The methods of obtaining that counsel are essentially two: circulating a paper or providing an oral presentation with suitable visual aids, or both. A situation audit may be addressed in either, or both, ways. The process may produce constructive and beneficial suggestions, but experience suggests that proposals for something new and different and possibly better often produce a negative reaction among peers, and often among superiors. There may be good and sufficient reasons for a negative reaction, such as the limitations of an organization's ability to finance and pursue the proposed option. Another possible cause for a negative reaction is a negative attitude toward change. The learned Bertrand Russell commented that governments (and, by implication, all organizations) have room for only one major idea at a time. Within an organization, the NIH ("not invented here") factor and the emotions of jealousy and fear that the proposal may raise the proposer's standing come into play In the world at large, think of Copernicus and Galileo and their concept that the earth revolved around the sun; the derision regarding "Fulton's Folly" (the invention of the steam boat); resistance to the idea that man might be able to fly; or the learned scientist who is said to have advised President Franklin Roosevelt that an atomic bomb could not be built. Persons who propose something new and different must be emotionally and intellectually prepared for negative reactions and, if necessary, be willing to persist and accumulate support. The commentators may be motivated more by traditional thinking, self-interest, and established practice than by openness and receptivity to innovation. The selection of reviewers who will fairly appraise the matter before them therefore becomes important, as does fairly evaluating - and, if appropriate, disregarding - negative comments.

THE NEXT STEP

This chapter has introduced some methods to reach the level of understanding that supports a confident decision. In this and the two preceding chapters, we have examined structured approaches that identify the kinds of information and assumptions we need to support particular well-defined decisions. We turn now to the difficult tasks of selecting relevant and valid information from the enormous flow of the irrelevant and ambiguous, in selecting assumptions where we must, and in reasoning from our accepted store of information and assumptions. These are fields of thought that have engaged some of the best human minds for centuries. Although our situation is made more difficult by the so-called "information explosion," they have addressed the matter of "how humans know" from many standpoints, and they have left us with an enduringly relevant body of thought. Our contemporaries continue that work. We turn to that general body of thought to illuminate our own, particular, decision-making endeavors.

Chapter 4

Thinking About Thinking

SCHOOLS OF THOUGHT

An Excursion into Isms

Thinkers have thought a lot, written a lot, about thinking, or reasoning, or what we know or can know. As usual, the Greeks provided a name for it: epistemology, the study of the sources, the nature, and the limits of human knowledge. The store of philosophical literature addressing the question of what we can know, and what we can infer from what we can know, has been accumulating for several thousand years, and it continues to grow. Concluding that one knows, or does not know, is in itself a very important decision within a decision making process, because our level of confidence in the relevant body of knowledge influences the final decision. We must therefore seek out some parts of that large body of thought that may be widely relevant to our own times and situations. What should be the face and mind that our conceptual good decision-maker turns toward her own search for the knowledge and understanding relevant to those conditions? A very brief excursion into some of the host of "isms" in philosophical thought introduces the range of choices. Let's begin with empiricism, which is essentially the basis of scientific method.

Empiricism has two related doctrines: 1) that most or all human knowledge derives from experience; 2) that most or all human concepts derive from experience. In everyday life, both doctrines are based on seeing, feeling, hearing, tasting, smelling. In scientific endeavor, both are based on hypotheses to be confirmed or discredited by experimentation and/or observation. The fundamental concepts of empiricism thus led to the division of science into separate disciplines and to the use of experiments and/or observation to confirm or refute hypotheses.

Pragmatism, a related theory, also emphasizes experience over *a priori* reasoning, but is perhaps best perceived as an alternative or enlarged interpretation of empiricism, arising from a very different view of "truth." The decision-making methodology outlined in earlier chapters could arguably be classified as pragmatism, although I believe it falls under the larger rubric of "modern rational empiricism." We must therefore devote a bit more attention to pragmatism and a few other philosophical approaches, with particular attention to pragmatism's concept of truth.

The general view of truth, certainly incorporated in "modern rational empiricism" is correspondence with external reality. For the pragmatist, "truth" lies in deciding how to solve practical problems and putting that decision into action. If the action solves the problem, the belief was true and the decision was correct. This approach applies to all actions: scientific experiments, solutions to problems of any kind, development of strategies and policies. The philosophical argument for this view was set forth by its influential proponent William James (1842–1910).

A brief visit with James' Lecture II, *What Is Pragmatism*, may illuminate pragmatism not only as a philosophical school of thought but also as a means for making practical decisions. I condense his argument. He asserted that the pragmatic method of resolving metaphysical disputes (concerning a reality that lies beyond what is perceptible to the senses) among philosophers was to assess the practical consequences of any particular belief. James held that pragmatism incorporates the empiricist attitude, but avoids abstraction, insufficiency, *a priori* reasons, fixed principles, closed systems, pretended absolutes and origins. Instead, it stresses concreteness, facts, adequate knowledge (not knowing everything, but knowing enough to act) and action. Pragmatism, he held, limbers up theories and puts them to work. The true value of an idea is a function of its consequences. The true is both what is good to believe and good for definite results. Truth "happens" to an idea, it is "made true" by events. Pragmatism thus rejects Descartes rationalism (see below) in favor of empiricism, knowledge gained by human experience. It simply sets aside, as lacking practical value, other theories of knowledge: idealism, phenomenalism (the theory that all knowledge is related to phenomena), and all other philosophical schools that perceive ultimate objective truth as unattainable. Pragmatism, James held, does not stand for any special results. It is simply a methodology, with no dogmas, no doctrine, no first principles or categories or supposed necessities. It looks instead to facts, consequences, results.

Positivism, which has various forms, is a close relative of empiricism and pragmatism in adhering to experience data and "scientific method." In marked contrast, rationalism, as advocated by its prestigious proponent René Descartes (1596–1650), holds that reason illuminates universally applicable basic axioms and enables one to deduce specific consequences from them. Rationalism holds that such axioms are self-evident, beyond doubt, independent of experience, and immune to the possibility of being proved false by experience.

Intuitionism refers to a method based on neither experience nor the senses. Intuitionism holds that humans have a way of "knowing" separate from experience or reasoning. I introduce it here merely to advance the discussion, and return to it later.

Although we have very thinly skimmed a very large subject, this necessarily all-too-brief survey has addressed the major choices available to contemporary decision-makers. The different views represent two distinct schools of philosophical thought, one (the *a posteriori*) based on or dependent upon experience, the other (the *a priori*) prior to or independent of experience. (The term "experience" as used here refers to the entire body of experience of mankind, rather than solely to an individual's experience.) It seems clear to me that both experience and reasoning must be employed, that "facts" must conform to external reality, that assumptions must sometimes be employed when facts are not available, that one must be very diligent in accepting either alleged facts or assumptions as bases for decisions, and that intuition in its broader "life experience" sense cannot be disregarded. For those reasons, it seems useful to employ a combination of critical judgment and structured method, which can be subsumed under the rubric of critical thinking, critical realism, or a variety of other terms. Critical thinking appeals because it implies receptivity to new information and differing opinions, coupled with intent and ability to detect flaws in information and assumptions and argumentation. These elements of thought can be subsumed under the heading of "modern rational empiricism." I explore it further below.

What is Critical Thinking?: The Founding Fathers

Socrates. One could perhaps go back to the earliest known writings of man and find examples of critical thinking, but Socrates (499-369 B.C.E.), who wrote nothing, and whose teaching is known only through the writings of his followers and contemporaries, is generally regarded as having established the use of critical reasoning, or philosophical dialogue, as a standard for Western philosophy. After serving with some distinction as a soldier in early adult life, then working as a stonemason, Socrates inherited enough wealth to support himself and his family, and devoted the remainder of his life to critical examination of the validity of popular opinions, particularly with respect to morality and virtue: "the good." He held forth in public places, addressing the upper stratum of the youth of Athens. His method was essentially dialectical, employing careful questioning of the bases for widely held doctrines, and by that method essentially demonstrating their weak plausibility. He is said to have turned the sophists' methods of petty critical questioning, perhaps appropriately described in modern terms as "nitpicking," to a constructive purpose. He offered no alternatives to the doctrines he addressed: his objective was to make his audience aware of the weaknesses in their beliefs, expressed in his comments that the only true wisdom lies in knowing that you know nothing, and that true wisdom comes to us only when we realize we know little about ourselves, the world around us, and life. His success in deflating accepted doctrine drew the attention and wrath of the political authorities, who charged and convicted him of corrupting the youth of Athens and interfering in its religion, and sentenced him to death. He rejected the efforts of his friends to escape imprisonment, on the ground that an individual citizen cannot be justified in disobeying the laws of the state even when they result in injustice.

Socrates provided something useful for us. First, he demonstrated the power of critical reasoning and absolute commitment to truth. He employed the dialectical method, in which one participant expresses an opinion or advances a proposition or resolution, and the respondent then inquires as to the reasoning or evidence that would support the statement. This is the method of logical argumentation or rational dialogue, examined later in this chapter and briefly earlier, and of scientific inquiry and experimentation. In the latter, scientists and scholars publish the results of their research or experimentation, others then conduct further work to verify the claimed results. If the work is validated and accepted, a new paradigm or hypothesis emerges, and the process continues. Socrates may not have invented the method, but his use of it established it as a powerful tool for advancing knowledge. Second, Socrates taught that we ought to be very careful about what we believe, and revealed that we often accept, and place in our mind as settled fact, convictions that cannot withstand critical examination. Third, Socrates argued that there is nothing permanent in human affairs, and therefore one should avoid euphoria in good times and depression in bad times. By implication, one should be prepared for change, and adapt to it. Fourth, Socrates established or furthered, in Western culture, the enduring philosophical study of "virtue": that is, of the characteristics or dispositions that are generally perceived as admirable and as distinguishing good people from bad.

A fifth and surely unintended lesson may be drawn from the example of Socrates' life, and his death. It bears repeating that human institutions, such as our contemporary governments, religious organizations, corporations, military forces, and a host of others are held together by a set of widely shared and strong beliefs, "the myths" which may or may not be objectively true. The leaders of the institutions perceive a critical inquiry into the validity of the myth as a threat to the organization's stability and purpose, and perhaps to their own positions and influence, and do not look favorably upon the inquiries and inquirers. It is very difficult to dislodge existing beliefs from our own store of beliefs, and certainly difficult to introduce the new and different to a larger body if it challenges the established organizational culture. (Pragmatism would argue that beliefs that benefit their holders and society in general are true because their consequences are beneficial.)

A final lesson: Socrates' ground for refusal to consider avoiding his death sentence by escape - that a citizen can never be justified in refusing to obey the laws of the state - might well have been undermined by the same critical scrutiny and reasoning he employed elsewhere.

We now fast forward roughly two thousand years, to another philosopher in another era, that of the last four hundred or so years that has seen the great explosion of human knowledge and its practical applications.

Descartes. I noted above that René Descartes has long been viewed as the most influential advocate of reasoning to attain a larger understanding of truth than that wholly derived from experience and observation. Nevertheless, he was a strong practitioner of critical thinking, and a great and enduring influence on its practice, not only on philosophy but also on the general advancement of knowledge. How much he may have been influenced by earlier philosophers one cannot know, but he is said to have leaped over Aristotle and medieval philosophers and his views on knowledge align with those of Socrates. He began from a position of utter skepticism, holding that he knew nothing and what he thought he knew was probably erroneous. Descartes employed his utter skepticism to prove to himself that he existed: that is, to differentiate fact from opinion. His famous phrase *Cogito, ergo sum* (I think, therefore I am) has often been criticized for carrying doubt much too far, but it served his method of stripping himself of "all past beliefs." Descartes argued that if some power were trying to deceive him into believing that he existed when he did not, he would have to exist in order to be deceived. He saw his "I am" conclusion not as a result of prior knowledge or experience data or a process of reasoning, but as springing intuitively and therefore unquestionably true. But, one might reasonably ask, what does his work imply for our contemporary world?

Descartes was seeking to develop a methodology that would enable him to avoid errors in the entire process of seeking knowledge and discovering new knowledge. He was seeking a method that worked for him, rather than proposing a universal method, but he published the *Discourse on Method* (1637) and his *Meditations on First Philosophy* (1641) to share what had in fact worked for him. His first principle was "never to accept anything as true unless I recognized it to be evidently such." Consider the relevance of that principle to, for example, our contemporary attribution of global warming to human activities over the last few centuries, after some 18,000-plus years of warming. His second principle was "to divide each of the difficulties which I encountered into as many parts as possible, and as might be required for an easier solution."[3] This principle is embodied in the "factors bearing on the problem" approach outlined in the opening chapters of this book. Its essence consists of breaking the problem (or, if one prefers, the matter being addressed) down into its several parts, analyzing each and the joint effects of those that are interlinked, then proceeding from the parts to the whole. Descartes' "third principle" was "to think in an orderly fashion, beginning with the things which are simplest and easiest to understand, and by degrees reaching toward more complex knowledge, even treating as though ordered materials which were not necessarily so." This principle is embodied in the contemporary concept of proceeding from the simple to the complex. Descartes last principle was "always to make enumerations so complete . . . that I would be certain nothing was omitted."[4] Or, leave no stone unturned, no option or consequence unconsidered.

As Descartes perceived, his rigor with respect to both facts and reasoning may set an unattainable standard for many practical situations and problems that might engage readers of this book. As he also perceived in publishing his method, his work may also have wide relevance. In particular, his first principle has high relevance in a period when the daily flow of information contains much that cannot withstand critical examination. I return to this phenomenon in the following paragraphs.

PROBLEMS OF INFORMATION QUALITY

True, False, or Just Doubtful?

Are the counsels of Socrates and Descartes relevant to our times and situation? Perhaps both of them required a rigor that is excessively demanding and impracticable in contemporary conditions, but their counsel to be careful of what we accept as useful fact certainly remains valid.

It has been said that our era has seen an "explosion of knowledge," or an "information explosion." It may be even more insightful to perceive the explosion as one of information that may or may not represent knowledge.

Most of what we "know" of contemporary life and events comes from exposure to the "media" for mass communication: television, radio, newspapers and news magazines, advertisements, sports events, internet sites, blogs. News and opinion shows and commentary and discussion groups are designed to attract a wide audience. They are produced and conducted by persons with the biases we have earlier noted, and by nature they are then selective in what they offer. Their commercial interests lie in attracting as many readers or viewers or listeners (fitting certain criteria) as possible, and that requires emphasis on the unusual and entertaining. The product has therefore been aptly termed "infotainment." The amount of space that can be devoted by newspapers and news magazine to any particular subject is limited. The amount of time that television and radio can devote to it is limited. The sheer volume and variety are so great that the information professionals who provide the information ordinarily have limited understanding of what is important in the matter being portrayed. Thus, some topics may get too much attention, some too little. Topics of local interest, or concerning popular fads or celebrity persons, often receive far more attention than much more important news of distant events. Complicated topics often get superficial treatment. For example, the media often feature gatherings of protesters, with well-prepared signs, garments featuring some message, leaders with bull horns directing the protesters. The media treatment often goes no further than video and sound coverage of the event (by television) and a press account of it with an estimate of the numbers of participants. Leaving the matter there may foster the impression that the protesters somehow appeared spontaneously. This information might be more meaningful to the reader-decision maker if the coverage extended to the who, what, when, where, how, and why aspects: who organized and paid for the event, what motivated the organizers, where the protesters were domiciled, how and where the protesters were recruited and whether and by whom were they paid, how their activities were orchestrated and by whom, who transported them to and from the protest site, and from where and by what means,

In all cases, the decision-makers for the media select, from a huge flow of potential material, that which will capture attention and fit the space or time available AND their own preferences and views. Guests on television talk shows are often introduced as "experts," and brought in because they are well known and thus have drawing power, without questioning their level of expertise or special knowledge of the current topic. "News" programs and exhibits are notoriously and openly "liberal" or "conservative," or perhaps religious or partisan on other grounds, and their content is shaped to appeal to a sympathetic audience. Programs featuring television personalities select persons to interview according to the contemporary story of interest or, with respect to larger issues, the program decision-makers' views. Persons who are known to differ may be invited, often with the apparent purpose of challenging or discrediting their views. The interviewer becomes part of the story, and his/her views may merely express a difference or go to some length to discredit the guest's views. Political advertising, and media support of particular candidates or issues, are best understood in the context of product advertising. Candidates are "packaged" to provide wide appeal, and presented in much the manner of consumer product "brand" advertising. Congressional committees may select witnesses whose views are known to be similar to the committee's majority. Governments at all levels engage in some measure of "managing" the news. A number of "Centers," so-called "think tanks," firmly support particular "causes," which are often grounded in "myths" for which proof is lacking or impossible to attain. "Good" names are created for them, to project the image of standing for some laudable purpose, which indeed some do. They are, nevertheless, advocates, and one cannot expect from them an unbiased consideration of matters within their range of interests.

The continuing information flow from the traditional mass communication media and "study" organizations is, then, not a shining example of a rigorous search for truth: "All media are to some extent guilty of distortions and omissions."[5] Although a number of instances of deliberate fabrications by reporters employed by major media outlets have been exposed in recent times, the more general problem lies in the nature of the news gathering and disseminating business. Reporters or researchers conscientiously seeking to learn the truth and inform us of it are subject to difficulties in obtaining and verifying essential information, selecting and discarding from the body of information they obtain, drawing their own inferences amid dealing with their own biases, and accommodating the preferences of their editors and the flow of other information competing for publication. In some of the print media, mistakes that appear in prominently displayed stories may be corrected, if at all, in a less conspicuous fashion.

In summary, in any communication system, there is a ratio of "signal" (the useful content) to "noise" that obscures and distorts. The "noise" may have many origins: bias of suppliers of information, lack of diligence, lack of understanding of the subject matter, misinterpretation, time and space constraints, passage through a number of nodes, deliberate deception, special pleading, conflicting accounts, fallacies, falsehoods, innuendo, out of context, outdated, overtaken by events, fragmented, based on hearsay, influenced by "bandwagon" or "follow the leader" effect. When any or some of these influences are present, the likely result is a distorted portrayal of the contemporary "state of nature." British Prime Minister Tony Blair, in a speech days before the end of his tenure, described the British media's posture with respect to government and politics as that of "a feral beast," that "saps the country's confidence and self-belief" and "reduces our capacity to take the right decisions . . ." The editor of the Observer newspaper called the speech "highly perceptive' and reflective of matters "being discussed constantly in newspaper and media offices all over the land."[6] While these comments were directed at the British media, they reflect similar competitive conditions and parallel concerns with respect to American media.

All this being said, one cannot turn away from the mass communication media, because they are vital to the process of constant refreshment and "creative destruction" and renewal of our mental data base. But, because their work is so important, mass media products must be viewed selectively and with a very strong skepticism. The need for verification by carefully selecting and diversifying our media sources is clearly indicated, as is recourse to other, more specialized sources that provide greater depth and expertise. Recall that Descartes "first rule" was "never to accept anything as true unless I recognized it to be evidently such: that is, carefully to avoid precipitation and prejudgment, and to include nothing in my conclusions unless . . . there was no occasion to doubt it." If one allows for necessary exceptions, and conscious substitution of explicit assumptions where uncertainty cannot be removed, Descartes' standard remains widely applicable.

To what sources, other than the traditional mass media, should one turn? The Internet offers a tremendous body of easily accessible and valuable information, but it is afflicted with problems both additional and similar to those of the older mass media, into whose realm it is increasingly expanding. *The Economist* of April 22, 2006 provided "A Survey of New Media" that explored the difficulty of verifying information posted on the Internet. As an example, it cites a study by *Nature* magazine "to compare the accuracy of a sample of articles drawn from Wikipedia [an online encyclopedia that publishes articles provided free of charge by contributors] and the Encyclopedia Britannica respectively."[7] The study found that the Wikipedia articles contained 162 errors, the Britannica articles 123 errors. After *Britannica* challenged, and *Nature* rebutted, *Britannica* issued a statement saying "our model, although not perfect, is the best." Moral: if one can't trust the distinguished old *Britannica* or the upstart but very large and widely consulted *Wikipedia*, whom can one trust? Certainly one cannot rely on all the blogs and other sources of the Internet, where verification is infeasible.

"Science," or scientific knowledge, seems a good bet, and it is on topics where knowledge is certain or nearly so, but one must also recognize a number of difficulties when an essentially scientific issue becomes a public policy issue. Scientists are far from unanimous on many scientific matters, and most of the "scientific" information widely publicized as a basis for policy decisions comes through the mass communication media and the advocacy "Centers," which may shape the state of scientific inquiry according to their own biases. Moreover, "science" as a unified whole, as a body of people and organizations all of one mind and intellectually equipped to form "scientific" judgments on any matter within the purview of any scientific field, exists only in the vocabularies of persons attempting to employ "scientific" opinion for their own purposes. Becoming, and being, a "scientist" demands much effort and dedication to one scientific field, and conversely entails the opportunity cost of not having time and preparation for judging matters outside that field. A prominent current example lies in the "scientific community's" reported differences on "global warming": its causes, potential consequences, and what mankind should do about it. This "scientific" question has now become a political and public policy issue, with each side able to find opinions they like, including many provided by "scientists" in unrelated fields. An example from recent years, in another arena of public policy, is provided by the "scare" publicity of so-called "scientific" consumer advocacy groups opposing food irradiation, and asserting (incorrectly) that the World Health Organization and the American Medical Association did not approve of irradiation. Although ultimately unsuccessful in prohibiting the process for use in the United States, the opposition delayed the present extensive use of irradiation to reduce the risk of food poisoning, in spite of the support of irradiation by the American Medical Association and the Food and Drug

Administration.[8] Unfounded claims to be "scientific" constitute a prominent form of the "appeal to authority" technique to defend a proposition. Perhaps the ultimate example, which unfortunately had to be disproved in practice, was the claim that Communism was "scientific socialism."

An important problem of public perception lies in properly distinguishing "knowing" from "hypothesizing." Much of what is publicly viewed as scientific "knowledge" is understood by working scientists as hypothesis, reflecting judgments reached from the set of verifiable facts available but subject to change as new facts become available. Until early in the Twentieth Century, a common assumption, regarded as knowledge, was that the location of land masses on the earth was fixed. A number of "scientists" had long recognized the apparent "fit' of separated land masses to each other, but the power and prestige of senior scientists delayed, for many years, acceptance of the theories of continental drift and plate tectonics. That stance in turn delayed progress in understanding earthquakes and other seismic activity. Copernicus and Galileo (and probably others) had concluded, from telescopic observations and calculations, that the earth revolved around the sun, but that conclusion was denied circulation because it challenged the Christian (Aristotelian) dogma of an earth-centered universe.

In summary, before accepting any claim on the argument that it is based on "science," one would wish to know both precisely what knowledgeable scientists in the field believe, and why they believe it. The mass media ordinarily do not provide these data, and often - as in the case of global warming allegedly due to man's activities - become strongly polarized in favor of one view or the other.

Statistics provide valuable, often indispensable information, but they can also be misused, misinterpreted, unreliable, direct or indirect, selectively designed to produce a specific conclusion, based on insufficient and/or improper samples, or accurate but used to support conclusions that are not justified. The terms "survey" and "averages" are particularly bandied about loosely. I have today received a marketing letter urging me to telephone for information, on the ground that "In a recent survey, new xx xxx customers reported average annual savings of more than $500." The questions concerning such a statement are many, including: who paid for the survey, who conducted it, who was surveyed; what were the questions; how were the questions posed, how was the average calculated? If there was a monetary saving, was it for the same quality of product or service? What percentage of callers gained nothing and did not become "customers?" The use and misuse of statistics are a very large subject, well beyond the confines of time, space, and purpose that constrain us here. Let it suffice, then, to note that statistics can be used selectively to support a wide variety of conclusions and decision options, and they are often used to produce a desired result.

What about information originating in one's own organization? Apart from the fact that information gathering and reporting in an organization are subject to many of the problems cited above with respect to the information media, consider again the fact that every little box on an organization chart represents an actual "store or forward" node in the organization's communication system. Consider also that there is an inherent problem with the organization as a communications system: managers do not like to report bad news to their superiors, the superiors do not like to receive such news; employees do not like to receive bad news regarding the state of the organization's health and prospects, and the senior management does not like to disseminate such news. The flow of information upward and downward is, moreover, shaped and repackaged at the "nodes." Bad news may travel slowly, if at all, and receive beauty treatment as it progresses. Good news - "good" in the sense that it is welcome, perhaps not good in the sense that it is valid - gets around expeditiously. The Internet and the organization's "intranet" may also produce much noise relative to signal, too irrelevant and too much. Perhaps most importantly, an organization, like a person, has beliefs and a sense of what it is. Any information that challenges those beliefs is likely to be unwelcome.

Faced with all the difficulties sketched above, what should our decision-maker do? First, recognize that rich and valuable sources of information, such as the Internet, are often imbedded in minefields of misinformation, disinformation, obfuscation, various other errors, and sheer overload of volume. It is clearly appropriate to incorporate a strong element of scepticism into one's decision-making mode. One need not and should not accept at face value any statement or body of information that is to be used in making a decision. All assertions or claims require validation. On the other hand, certainty may be inordinately expensive. The requirement is to find and verify what might be termed "operational truth": that is, relevant and sufficiently near certainty to serve the intended purposes. "Operational truth" is ordinarily available with effort, as "signal" to be extracted from the massive stream of "noise."

Some highlighting of the longer-term implications of this discussion may be useful. So, let's return to some earlier comments. To reiterate: we humans, as individuals and organizations, bring to the decision-making occasion the sum of our experience, education, convictions, moral and ethical values, principles, biases, regional values. I had also observed that conscious development of a **decision-making mode** and a conscious switch into it when significant decision-making occasions arise should improve our performance. It follows that our **decision-making mode** requires constant development, creative destruction of invalid old beliefs, and guarded acceptance of new information and beliefs. We are, perforce, consciously and unconsciously structuring and restructuring the fund of stored information and belief that we bring to decision-making. Since some, often most, of the information relevant to the decision at hand is stored in our own memory, it should be useful to decide what information we need for our personal and occupational responsibilities, to identify information sources that are reliable and relevant, and to employ those sources consistently over long periods. Surely the quality of our mental store of information is reflected in the quality of our decisions. In turn, the quality of our store of information depends upon the quality of our reading, viewing, listening, and selecting our sources of information.

The moral: take care to assure that what is added to one's store of knowledge is knowledge.

We turn now to the employment of information in thought processes.

TOOLS OF THE TRADE

Induction

Descartes' methods of reasoning from a part to a whole, from the simple to the complex, and from the particular to the general, may be subsumed under the general process of induction. Induction is based upon data derived from experience. It allows one to derive a general conclusion from a number of particular observations, experiments, and more recently from samples and surveys. Later thinkers, such as John Locke in his *Essay Concerning Human Understanding*, moderated Descartes' skepticism by highlighting the important point that inductive methods provide a degree of probability, rather than certainty. The most familiar example is our unquestioned belief that the sun will rise from the east tomorrow, because it has done so on every morning experienced by humans. That experience justifies our confidence, but it does not provide certainty that an event that has not occurred cannot occur. In fact, a number of theoretical occurrences - all with, as far as we can know, very low probability - could cause it to rise elsewhere, or not at all.

Thus, induction requires one to believe that there is a high probability that the phenomena we have observed in the past will continue in the same manner in the future. As a reasoning tool, it can suggest hypotheses that may then be tested. It cannot "prove" a hypothesis, but it can provide an inference of probability. It cannot eliminate the possibility that other hypotheses, not yet recognized, may exist.

John Stuart Mill (1806–1877 or 1878) provided us four basic methods for the use of induction that remain valid. They are practical, and the brief discussion of them below may be useful for anyone seeking sources of causation. The "Method of Agreement" carefully examines all the circumstances in all the instances of the phenomena being investigated, and identifies circumstances that they have in common. The causation lies in the common circumstances, and if there is only one common circumstance one may conclude that it is the cause or effect of the phenomena being investigated. A familiar historical example is the tracing of the source of a cholera outbreak to a single well, by identifying the use of that well by cholera victims as the common factor. The "Method of Difference" examines instances in which the phenomena being investigated occur, and instances in which it does not occur, and if they have every circumstance in common except one, which occurs only in the former, the circumstance in which the two instances differ is the effect or the cause or a part of the cause of the phenomenon. The two methods can be used together, as in the case of the cholera outbreak, and are commonly employed in control group experiments. The "Method of Residues" subtracts anything known to be the effect of known antecedents, and the "residue" is the effect of the remaining antecedents. In other words, subtract what is already established, and concentrate the search on the remaining data. The "Method of Concomitant Variation" examines the relationship of two phenomena that consistently vary together in some way, i.e., when one varies, the other also varies, directly or inversely. If this relationship exists, one is either a cause of the variation of the other, or is connected through some element of causation.

Induction is an everyday tool in our lives. It is the basis for ways of thinking based upon experience and observation. We live under the assumption that the future will be like the past: our jobs, our homes, our way of life will be there tomorrow. Probably so, maybe not: induction can provide only probability, addressed in the paragraphs below.

Deduction

In contrast to induction with its varying degrees of probability, deduction—proceeding from the general to the particular—provides certainty: if the premises are true, the conclusion is necessarily true, a probability of one. The most used example is the syllogism, and the most used example of the syllogism is:

"All men are mortal,

Socrates is a man,

therefore Socrates is mortal."

The syllogism consists of a major premise, a minor premise, and a conclusion. In the example above, "All men are mortal" is the major premise, "Socrates is a man" is the minor premise, and "therefore, Socrates is mortal" is the conclusion. If either the major premise or the minor premise of a syllogism is untrue, the conclusion is untrue. Its probability is zero. It follows, then, that both premises must be thoroughly verified. It seems illogical, but it is nevertheless true, that the process of deduction depends on establishing major premises by the process of induction. Mankind has observed that every human, without exception, dies: hence, the "major" premise "all men are mortal," which is a general statement followed by the two particular statements "Socrates is a man" and "therefore Socrates is mortal."   Syllogisms and other features of "formal logic" provide useful, often indispensable, tools for scientific and intellectual inquiry and engineering design, but have little utility for ordinary decision making and argumentation. In contrast, "informal logic," which is addressed later in this chapter, has great utility.

Intuition: A Sometime Thing

In one formal sense and in common usage, "intuition" refers to the phenomenon of knowing or acting without knowledge acquired by ordinary observation or inference or study. Intuition is also often viewed in the "heart versus mind" context, as exemplified in the various assertions to the effect that the heart has reasons the mind cannot know. In matters of romance, that assertion has a certain ring of truth, but even there the history of human affairs advises us to turn on the **Decision Making Mode** switch. We encounter cases in which contemporary popular media and popular figures and some managers urge that we develop our capacity for intuition and let it guide our decision making: all on the basis, itself intuitive, that there is some hidden source of reason or wisdom that we can draw upon increasingly if only we will.

Certainly intuition is inherent in our mental processes. We are forced to rely on it when we must act without time for fact-finding and deliberation. It is also true that thought and calculation can occur subconsciously. We often express thoughts in conversations without having consciously decided upon what to say. Moreover, we conduct many motor functions without thought, as in sports where the baseball player swings at the pitch or the basketball player takes the shot without reflection. We drive our automobile without thinking about how to drive an automobile.

On the other hand, intuition is an uncertain and unreliable guide. It lacks or abjures means to assess the probability of being correct. It can serve as an excuse for failure to perform due diligence. It is the parent of the "snap judgment" and "hasty generalization." It ignores the potential of rigorously defining and limiting the problem, gathering facts, applying critical thinking and reasoning, employing dialogue and informed dissent, assessing probabilities, and all the other techniques that are time-proven and available. It breeds excessive confidence in those who employ it. Adolf Hitler's famous "intuition" led Germany first to success, and shortly thereafter into a disastrous war. British Prime Minister Neville Chamberlain's intuitive assessment that Hitler could be trusted to keep his word (because he had given it "to me") in the infamous Munich Agreement, enabled the German dictator to continue Germany's course of aggression and expansion. The Japanese leadership entered its period of aggression and war with the United States on the basis of an intuitive assessment that the United States would not have the will to recover from early defeats. The United States suffered the successful surprise Japanese attack on Pearl Harbor apparently because of an intuitive belief that the Japanese would attack elsewhere. One could cite innumerable other examples.

Although intuition of the nature we are considering here is not by itself a reliable tool for serious decision-making, it nevertheless offers options. When we must make an immediate decision, and have nothing else to go on, we must "go with our gut." When the decision need not be immediate, intuition provides a starting point for the decision making process, essentially not going beyond some insight into the existence of a problem or matter requiring attention, definition, and further study. Intuition, in this sense of the term, can usefully inform us to switch to **Decision-making Mode.**

However, in another sense with respected credentials, and as we have earlier observed, "intuition" may provide the final step in the process of reasoning. In that "go - no go" final step, we reach a conclusion on the basis of all our experiences and knowledge, rather than only the knowledge recently gained by a particular process of fact-finding and reasoning. Intuition, in this sense, draws upon our entire life experience and knowledge of the world and human behavior. It informs us that the reasoning process does or does not suffice. It determines whether the conclusion we are about to make meets the requirements: feasible, practicable, legal, moral, ethical and, on the whole, reasonable. That determination, in turn, depends upon what the decision maker perceives as feasible, practicable, legal, moral, ethical, and reasonable: what is stored in the decision maker's mental data base. As we have earlier observed, if we bring our accumulated store of knowledge and character to every significant decision, it behooves us to work continuously and consciously to enlarge and enhance these aspects of our decision making capability. That process requires the selection of reliable information sources that enhance and update our knowledge of our own occupation, of any other field of knowledge we hope to pursue, and of larger and enduring subjects relevant to our roles in life outside our occupations.

We learn from our own experience, of course, but the larger body of human experience enables us to draw upon the experience and insights of others. Good literature, which certainly includes good fiction, exposes us to the whole body of human experience. Serious contemporary periodicals and visual materials keep us current on contemporary "states of nature" and on matters of occupational interest. We have earlier pointed out that much of the strong flow of "infotainment" is useless or harmful "noise" that must be filtered out. That unyielding requirement for selectivity must also address the problem of fallacies in reasoning, because they, as well as falsehoods, distortions, and opinions disguised as facts, are often present in the flow of "infotainment."

Hypotheses

An hypothesis is, by definition, "A tentative assumption made in order to draw out and test its logical or empirical consequences" or "an assumption . . . made for the sake of argument " or "an interpretation of a practical situation or condition taken as a ground for action." An hypothesis employed "to draw out and test" the consequences of a proposed option or to interpret "a practical situation" can be very useful in suitable circumstances. In ordinary terms, an hypothesis is a "what if" or "if, then" question, a "tentative assumption" that some particular "state of nature" other than the existing or perceived one exists or did exist or will exist, employed to examine what consequences that state of nature may have for the matter under consideration.   An hypothesis differs from an assumption in that assumptions are acted upon as if they were established facts. Hypotheses are useful methods of discovery and of verification. A postulate (a statement assumed to be true) is developed, and then subjected to some test to determine its truth or falsity. Although an hypothesis may be useful in merely calling attention to a possibility, and thus opening a line of inquiry, its practical value rests upon its testability.

Formulating a useful and testable hypothesis requires both knowledge and imaginative thinking. The process has served the advancement of science for centuries: for example, Newton's great work on optics and gravitation (among his other great achievements) progressed through hypotheses confirmed by experiments. About two hundred years later, Einstein advanced Newton's work with his General Theory of Relativity, an hypothesis that was later confirmed experimentally with observations of light passing near the sun during a solar eclipse. In military affairs, hypotheses can provide clues to enemy intentions. A conspicuous example is the hypothesis postulated in World War II by Pacific Fleet intelligence personnel that an anticipated Japanese attack would be against Midway. Some of the code used by the Japanese Navy could be decoded by American intelligence services, and that work had shown that an attack was in preparation against an American position. The problem was that Japanese communications designated American-held positions by code words or characters, and the Pacific Fleet intelligence staff had not been able to link the designator for the coming attack to a particular place. To test the Midway hypothesis, U. S. Pacific Fleet planted a message from Midway, with high probability of its being intercepted and read by Japanese intelligence, stating that the island was short of water. Shortly thereafter, Japanese naval communications noted that a certain designator was short of water. The Pacific Fleet, already well aware of Japanese naval capabilities, was then confident that it knew the objective and approximate timing of the impending Japanese operation.[9]

The preceding example suggests the potential of hypotheses in other areas to narrow and focus the search for facts, by validation or negation. One postulates that something one is uncertain of is true, and reasons that if it is true certain events are occurring or certain conditions exist, and one designs tests to determine if the latter is true. However, this is an arena in which the fallacy of "affirming the consequent" (reversing the logical statement "If P, then Q" to "Q, therefore P") raises its ugly head. One could have inferred that the Japanese were engaged in a deception operation to focus American attention on Midway, in order to cloak the intent to attack elsewhere. A single hypothesis may suffice, but some situations may suggest the testing of all plausible and testable hypotheses. If several hypotheses are employed, it may be appropriate to treat them as one would treat decision options, by making a matrix of columns and rows, hypotheses arrayed by columns, notes on each hypothesis in each row. When due diligence has been performed, one employs the matrix to inform the decision or to conclude that the evidence is inconclusive.

Probabilities

Life offers few certainties. We live, work, and play in a milieu of probabilities. That being the case, everyone, and particularly every professional manager, will encounter situations in which some acquaintance with a few elements of this very large and complex subject will be useful in business and personal decisions. For our very limited purposes, and for those not already familiar with the subject, most of what we need to know can be briefly summarized. For any but simple occasions, one needs a strong knowledge of the subject or a qualified professional, in much the same manner as one can treat minor ills with home remedies but always retains the option of seeking the services of a physician.

Probabilities provide a way of expressing likelihood in numerical terms. They can be expressed as decimal numbers between zero and one (example, .75), or percentages (75%), or odds (3 to 1), or ratios (3/4). Expressing the probability as a decimal system number simplifies calculation of dependent probabilities. A decimal probability is, to repeat, a number between one and zero. The probability of an event and its complement (the probability that it will not happen) must therefore sum up to one. If an ultimate probability depends upon the probabilities of two or more preceding events, the ultimate probability is the product of the preceding probabilities. Thus, if in order to reach a desired payoff measure, several separate tasks must be accomplished, and we label those tasks x, y, and z, each with a probability of .9, the ultimate probability is .9 times .9 times .9, or .729.

The preceding sentence introduces the concept of *a priori* or "objective" probability. In contrast to the philosophical concept of the *a priori* as knowledge independent of experience, *a priori* probabilities are based on statistical analysis or mathematical certainty. Actuarial tables, derived from statistical data bases and used by insurance companies and other institutions, are familiar examples of statistical analysis. Mathematical certainty establishes gambling odds, such as the probability of drawing an ace from a deck of 52 cards that includes four aces. When probabilities for particular events or states of nature are known, and the return if the event does in fact occur is also known, they can be used to identify the expected value of each state of nature or option or combination of options. The decision maker then selects the option that best fits the decision criteria, usually the largest expected value. A further use lies in finding causation by reversing the process. If an event occurs and our data establish that 80 percent of all such events are caused by a certain equipment failure, we may hypothesize that the *a priori* probability of this event having the same cause is .8.

We now come to the controversial Bayesian "subjectivity" method, based upon the work of Thomas Bayes (1702–1761). If one does not know the "objective" probabilities of x, y, and z above, Bayesian methods allow use of "subjective" values: that is, what we think the probabilities are. Proponents of this usage assert that when one does not have "objective" probabilities (those derived from actual measurement or mathematical certainty), the method is a measure of one's opinion, or degree of conviction. An experienced person in most fields will have some opinion as to the likelihood of some event or proposition. Bayesian methods allow that opinion to be quantified. For example, a person with long experience in the stock market might state his belief that the Dow Jones average of thirty leading stocks will go up ten percent next year. If challenged to state how strongly he holds that belief, the expert might express it as "0.8 probability that the Dow Jones average will increase by 10% within the next year." Different persons would probably have different opinions and levels of confidence. Bayesian proponents believe that, properly understood, the subjective values assigned are legitimate and rational uses because they are expressions of the level of confidence of the person assigning them. "Subjectivists maintain that beliefs come in varying gradations of strength, and that an ideally rational person's graded beliefs can be represented by a *subjective probability function* **P**."[10] A further long-standing defense of the method lies in the assertion that subjectivity is also present in the assembling of "objective" data, and the Bayesian method makes the subjectivity explicit.

One would prefer to have and employ objective probabilities, but Bayesian "subjective" methods not only allow us to proceed under uncertainty but also to identify what we do not know but need to know, One may employ a statement or proposition employing subjective probabilities as an hypothesis, and then seek the data necessary to prove or disprove the statement. The use of subjective probabilities thus permits us to focus efforts to obtain objective probabilities or reduce the range of uncertainty. They may also inform us of what the probabilities have to be to achieve our aim in a particular case. For example, a developer wishes to create a waterfront condominium community in which the sale of a condominium residence will also permit the buyer to purchase a boat slip in a community docking facility. The developer learns that four organizations - the Coast Guard, the county government, the Port Authority, and the Corps of Engineers - must approve the project and grant permits. On the basis of the known policies of those organizations, he assumes the probabilities of approval of the facility as conceptually designed are: Coast Guard, 1.0; county 0.9, Port Authority. 0.75; Corps of Engineers, 0.5. Multiplying these probabilities, he obtains an estimated probability of .3375 that the proposal will be approved , and the complementary probability of .6625 that it will not be approved. He is then able to weigh three options: to seek approval of the project as planned, to abandon or defer the project, or to make design changes that will add to the cost but have a greater probability of approval.

Bayesian subjective probabilities can provide a very useful learning tool. This writer had, at one time, responsibility for an organization heavily involved in providing probabilities for the values employed in two mathematical models and various algorithms. We began with subjective probabilities, often developed by considerable periods of gazing at the ceiling, because objective probabilities were not known. Having identified specific gaps in the necessary knowledge, our parent organization was then able to set up repeated experiments to obtain "objective" data. The result was not only improved data, but also improvements in the parent organization's capabilities, because it identified specific needs for improvement.

On this experience and others, I estimate that the probability of improving one's knowledge by initially employing subjective probabilities in mathematical models, algorithms, and quick estimates is probably greater then 0.75. I further estimate that, when you have to go with what you've got, subjective probabilities have a probability greater than 0.5 of being useful. For matters of greater complexity or difficulty, I estimate that the probability that one needs an expert in probability and statistics is also greater than 0.5.

The Pareto Uncertainty Principle

The so-called Pareto Uncertainty Principle provides a potentially useful application of both *a priori* probability and the so-called "Murphy's Law." Vilfredo Pareto (1848–1923) was educated in mathematics and literature at the Polytechnic Institute in Turin, and was later employed as an engineer/mathematician for the Italian railroads. He remained very interested in economic policy, pursued that study and ultimately became head of economics at the University of Lausanne in 1893. In 1906 he published a mathematical formula observing that twenty percent of the Italian people owned 80 percent of the wealth. In the 1930's–1940's, Dr. Joseph Juran, who was one of the management "greats" and viewed as the originator of Quality (of product) Management, recognized what he considered as "the vital few and the trivial many," holding essentially that 20 percent of anything is responsible for 80 percent of the results. Applying this concept, he observed that 20 percent of the product defects cause 80 percent of the problems (or complaints). In a near-perfect example of the workings of Murphy's Law (if anything can go wrong, it will), this observation became known as the Pareto Principle, or the 80/20 rule, probably because Juran had referred to Pareto. Other commonplace aphorisms assert that some small minority of personnel in a project accomplish the majority of the results, or a few products out of many provide most of the profits.[11]

The 80/20 principle is, of course, an imprecise conclusion drawn from common experience. If one is dealing with results, as

Juran was, and there are many causes, common sense and observation inform us that some are more important than others. The old adage "First Things First" suggests that the general idea is both widely recognized and long established. Unfortunately, some urgency is often assigned to unimportant matters: they become "first" only because some time limitation has been arbitrarily placed upon them. Whatever one wishes to call it, the 80/20 concept reminds us to practice a kind of triage in our work, recognizing the need to allocate time and effort to maximize the return on time spent. When there are many choices regarding what to address, many decisions to make, it may be useful to list the choices in descending order of their probable payoffs (according to established or estimated payoff measures) and work downward from the top of the list. The 80-20 principle can steer us in the direction most likely to produce results.

Informal Logic and Argumentation

Informal logic as a method of reaching decisions by two or more people incorporates much of what has been outlined in this and preceding chapters. Properly understood and properly used, it is a powerful tool for group decision making. It is usefully defined as a method of "applying critical rules of good argument to argumentative discourse on controversial issues in natural language." It is an "essentially pragmatic endeavor" requiring the participants to employ "empathy, a critical perspective, careful attention to language, the ability to deal with vagueness and ambiguity, balanced recognition of the stronger and weaker points of . . . {an imperfect argument}, a careful look at the evidence behind a claim, the skill of identifying conclusions, sorting out the main line of argument from a mass of verbiage, and the critical acumen needed to question

claims based on expert knowledge in specialized claims or arguments."[12]

The word "argument" here implies a "claim," a statement
or proposition or resolution presented as a locus for discussion
and/or research, and "argumentation" refers to those processes.
"Thus every argument is conceived along the lines of a challenge-
response model or interactive dialogue, in which two people 'reason
together."[13]

The proponents of the "argument" have the obligation to provide all the reasons that support it. Those who believe otherwise
have a parallel obligation to explore thoroughly the proponents'
reasons, as well as the question the statement is intended to answer. Both advocates and opponents must provide evidence or reasons to support their positions, and both must be willing to accept
well-supported arguments advanced by the other. Argumentation
means, then, a cooperative search for truth or understanding via
"persuasion dialogue."

"Argument" as used in its ordinary sense implies strong emotions; loyalty to a particular part of the organization; defense of
"turf," status, power, influence; budgets; personal animosities; resistance to change, adherence to traditional thinking. The entry of
some of this into the deliberative process is often inevitable, but
seldom constructive. Discussions, oral and written, conducted in
this atmosphere, are essentially sterile, reminiscent of Shakespeare's
phrase, "full of sound and fury, signifying nothing."[14] They have a
place only in conditions in which special pleading is expected, the
advocates do not intend to convince their opponents, and decisions
are made by those viewing the argument rather than the proponents themselves Argumentation sharply contrasts with the ordinary meaning of argument. It refers to a cooperative effort to
reconcile opposing views, or to accept one entirely, or to develop

greater understanding. It is a discipline, growing out of traditional studies of rhetoric. It is taught at university undergraduate and graduate levels, with a long and important history and continuing research and development by scholars devoted to the subject. It is defined as "the study of effective reasoning." Obviously, we cannot here lay out the discipline in its entirety, but borrowing some of its principles may be both useful to our purpose and an encouragement for greater knowledge and use. What follows below is a brief summary of the more important principles, supplementing what has been noted above.

Argumentation is a process in which all parties cooperate in reaching judgments about matters that are uncertain and contingent. It is non-coercive. The work proceeds by using a single declarative sentence, a "resolution" defining an issue or controversy, as a locus for discussion. A resolution may concern facts, definitions, values, or policies. Issues are the questions inherent in the controversy, and vital to its resolution. Reducing a matter of considerable complexity to a single statement or resolution is not a trivial endeavor, and it may be necessary to identify and address a number of issues within the scope of the proposed measures. This is a form of the "factor analysis" mentioned in earlier chapters, and as many issues as necessary may be addressed. The advocate of any particular view bears the burden of proof with respect to that view, and must provide supporting argument and evidence. Opponents of that view bear the burden of rejoinder, with supporting arguments and evidence, to the arguments put forth by a particular advocate. This maintains continuity in the discussions. The burden of proof then shifts back and forth between proponents and opponents. Questions of fact are resolved not by argumentation and discussion, but by research and verification. Assumptions are recognized, accepted as such, and explicitly stated. Formal logic employing analytical or categorical syllogisms is not appropriate for discussions of this nature. The appropriate method is in a dialogue sifting out what is fact or probably fact, significant, relevant, and important to the matter from the fallacious and irrelevant. The dialogue continues until the focal point of disagreement, the *stasis* that defines precisely what is in dispute, has been identified and a judgment is reached with respect to the resolution.

The preceding paragraphs provide a bare introduction to a much larger, and very beneficial, discipline for organizational and group decision-making. Argumentation provides a set of rules, a process, for resolving differences of opinion and questions of fact and advancing toward true understanding. Its teaching and wide-spread adoption should be useful to any organization's management development program, as a means of reaching decisions through a widely understood, orderly process of deliberation, establishment of facts, selection and clear statement of assumptions, and reasoning together toward a decision fitting our criteria of feasible, practicable, legal, moral, ethical, and reasonable.

Dialogue As a Way of Thinking

The preceding discussion leads us to the use of dialogue in another manner Although "dialogue" is ordinarily understood as occurring between two or more persons, we can and do use dialogue with ourselves in pondering a problem or decision. Our ordinary weakness in this activity lies in failure to state a specific claim or resolution, preferably in writing: in other words, failure to provide a locus for argumentation. I believe it is ordinarily useful to structure the argument in a manner to permit posing a number of subsidiary issues. Employing the earlier example for an ordinary decision, consider the following proposition: "Resolved: I should buy a new car this month." This statement is deficient because it proposes a solution to a problem without describing the problem. The solution arises from a perceived need, which might be stated as "My present automobile is necessary to my livelihood, and is nearing the end of its economical life." One could then argue that a more appropriate definition of the issue would be: "Resolved, I should replace my current automobile this month." One could then proceed to a number of subsidiary issues. Do I really need to replace the current automobile? Why? This month? Why? If I do, should I replace it with a new vehicle, or a "pre-owned" one? Why? Is there an economic advantage in always procuring a pre-owned vehicle? If so, what make, what model, how old? Buy or lease? How much should I be prepared to pay? How do I avoid an excessive emotional attachment to a particular vehicle? How do changes in the probable use and users of the vehicle affect the decision? And so on. In this type of dialogue, the technique of "writing to find out what you think" may be very useful when considering significant decisions. Should I marry this person? Look for a different job? Look for a new career? Move to a different state? Pursue a particular degree? Make a major purchase?

Dialogue is, then, a form of critical thinking ordinarily but not necessarily involving two or more participants, a structured method for enhancing knowledge and understanding of a particular issue and the subordinate issues that it raises. The process ordinarily leads to a conscious decision to take some particular action or reach a particular conclusion. It is "argumentation" with oneself, in contrast to "argument," a subject sadly more commonly encountered in decision making, to which we now turn.

Argument From the Interests of the Parties

Special Pleading. Resolving an issue or a number of issues by cooperative argumentation as outlined above is a method to be desired and made the standard for group decision making. We have noted, however, that any significant human decision produces, or is perceived as likely to produce, advantage for some, disadvantage for others. The central issue is the same: "who gets what?" Senior management might wish that subordinate levels set aside their "turf" and "rice bowl" biases, and proceed in accordance with the rules of *argumentation* to a responsible conclusion representing the broader interests of the organization. Experience suggests, however, that managers are likely to perceive change as either beneficial or adverse to their departmental responsibilities, and therefore adverse to their interests. Their subordinates may have similar views. Decision makers must therefore expect some level, perhaps a high level, of *special pleading*, recognize it for what it is, and seek to control it and use it beneficially. *Special pleading* stresses reasons to pursue a particular option and neglects, omits, or distorts and downplays reasons not to pursue that option, or to prefer a different option.

Properly understood and openly represented for what it is, *special pleading* is a legitimate form of argument. It is not intended by the advocates on either side to change the opposition's opinion. It is, instead, aimed at influencing the judgments of a target decision-making audience. It is the ordinary procedure in criminal prosecutions and civil lawsuits and in all forms of marketing and salesmanship. In courtroom environments, *special pleading* is expected and recognized for what it is. The counter-parties offer their own arguments, and judges and/or juries decide which is the more persuasive. In election campaigns, candidates and their campaign organizations emphasize all the fine qualities of the candidate, and all the failings of the opposing candidates. The use of misinformation, disinformation, omitted information, irrelevant information, overweighted information, and outright false information is widely recognized as common in political campaigns, but it is also a common characteristic of the *special pleading* form of persuasion.

Appeal to the emotions is also a common characteristic, as is the use of logical fallacies. Let the decision maker beware.

Formal Debate. Special pleading is also the central feature of formal debate, in which each side argues for and against a specific proposition, cast in the form of a resolution. In these matters, the decision maker hears and sees arguments openly advocating and openly opposing a particular judgment, and decides according to her perception of the merits of those arguments. Debate is, then, by definition not a search by the debating principals for genuine understanding and truth. It allows for all the forms of twisted information, for appeals to the emotions, for the deliberate use of common fallacies.

Informal Debate. A process akin to formal debate may provide an opportunity to employ special pleading usefully, by allowing the various advocates to present and advocate their views, and seek to rebut the views of others, in a scheduled presentation or series of presentations before a decision maker. Such a process, which may also employ writings, provides the advocates their "day in court," and can provide the decision maker a rough measure of the intensity of emotion surrounding the issue. It may be a useful part of the decision maker's "due diligence." It also forces advocates to examine their positions critically and present the strongest plausible supporting arguments. It has the potential to relieve some of the tension, to sharpen the issues, to expose internal rivalries, and possibly to reach agreement. It also takes into account the possibility that advocacy and bias may be justified: being biased in favor of some particular option or viewpoint is not necessarily equal to being wrong. It allows for the possibility that an advocate can also be right for the wrong reasons, and it may expose legitimate dissatisfactions. The process provides a means for decision makers to resolve an issue or issues by scheduling a confrontation, or confrontations, of opposing views and those who hold them, followed by a conclusive decision. The decision may lead to a mellowing of tensions, a judgment by the losers that they have been fairly heard, and a general acceptance of the decision. In issues of great importance, where careers and power and prestige and compensation are affected, some advocates may continue to contest the decision. Some may leave the organization to seek solace and reward elsewhere, and some may continue opposition from within. From the standpoint of the organization, the departure or transfer of some personnel for greener pastures may be preferable to their continued opposition from within. For some individuals, the decision may have diminished their prospects in that organization and made it preferable to seek other opportunities. These possibilities fall within the categories of undesired and unforeseen consequences, and management should anticipate and be prepared to address them.

The Dangers of Debate. A danger of the formal or informal debate process is that the more persuasive case may be made by the more articulate and convincing *special pleader*, and result in the better case being defeated and the wrong decision made. People become attached to their views and identified with them. They have heard, and swept aside, the counter arguments, or refused to hear them. Opposition has strengthened their convictions. Some, perhaps a great deal, of that conviction comes through in their exposition of their case and may be persuasive to the listener. A formal debate case in point may have changed history: the famous - or, more properly, infamous - 1933 student debate of the Oxford Union, in which the affirmative won the debate over what Winston Churchill termed the "ever shameful resolution . . . That this house refuses to fight for King and country." Although the debate was clearly a student event, it concerned a highly charged and emotional issue affecting the lives of thousands or, in the event, millions, and it received worldwide publicity. Churchill continued that it was easy in England to laugh off this episode as a student folly, but it fostered a world view of "a divided, degenerate Britain." The effect was, in fact, palpable: Lord Lloyd, who was close to Italy's leader Mussolini, noted that the latter had been struck by the Oxford Union resolution, and "regarded Britain as a frightened, flabby old woman who . . . would only bluster and was, anyhow, incapable of making war."[13]

What conclusions may we infer from this discussion of decision-maker endorsed debate? First, it is clear that debate may be useful in developing and presenting the arguments for and against a particular option, but it also introduces a third element: the personality and emotional appeal of the most proficient special pleader. Debate cannot be dispassionate, and skilled debaters make no effort to make it so. High-priced attorneys do not command high prices entirely because of their more profound knowledge of the law: they are students of human emotions, students of the themes that may appeal to juries or particular judges, skilled at exploiting them, and users of the information media to influence public opinion with respect to their clients. The 1933 "Resolution" cited above is the classic example of an emotional appeal to an audience most receptive to it - those who would have to fight and perhaps die or suffer serious injuries in a future conflict - with the disastrous impact of having made that eventuality more likely. In summary, the results of debate may reflect more the skill and passion of the debaters than the merits of their case. The debater, one must recall, is seeking victory rather than truth. For that reason, those who must judge and decide the matter must beware of selecting the better persuader rather than the better case. But, properly understood as special pleading and employed in the service of sophisticated decision-makers, debate can be useful in identifying weak points and shaky "facts."

The Devil's Advocate Method

The "devil's advocate" method, which requires assignment of one or more persons as advocates of a viewpoint counter to the culture or prevailing viewpoint of an organization, or counter to a particular proposition, is a form of debate. It is not necessary when there are significant and open advocates for a different view. It has been used when the prevailing "climate of opinion" in an organization is so strongly favorable to a particular view that the organization's management decides that someone or some group must be designated to challenge it and argue for an alternative. In that application, the method has, in my view, all the failings of the formal or informal debate method, plus others. To begin: if a particular viewpoint is so strongly held in an organization that this step is thought necessary, it has become a part of the organization's "culture," closely connected to its reason to exist. It is unlikely that persons designated as "Devil's Advocate" have any enthusiasm for the task of opposing their own beliefs. Second, having been assigned to it, they are likely to believe that they have nothing to gain and much to lose by strong advocacy. Third, a vigorous presentation of the alternative view may serve only to harden support for the prevailing one: there must be an audience willing to be persuaded, and by definition such an audience does not exist in this situation. In one case with which this writer has direct acquaintance, an American official recommended that the head of a foreign country's military intelligence staff appoint a mid-grade officer to serve as "Devil's Advocate" for the cause of this particular nation's principal enemy. The appointment was made. Some months later I talked directly to the officer appointed. He informed me that he had become a pariah, that his colleagues regarded him as having gone over to the side of the enemy, that his career prospects were badly damaged, and that his advocacy had served only to harden the views which his appointment required him to challenge.

This episode provides, of course, only anecdotal evidence. It is conclusive only with respect to this particular case. It does not negate the possibility that the technique can be usefully employed in some situations. It does, however, suggest some of the dangers of the method when it is used to challenge the organization's set of central beliefs, essentially the core of what it lives by. If management has somehow come to view that culture as requiring questioning and perhaps change, an alternative method may lie in opening an inquiry by posing a series of questions for response by subordinate elements. This may constitute a somewhat abbreviated and muted situation audit, but it provides management's sanction for organizational self-examination and avoids placing the onus for challenging the organization's central beliefs on one person.

Writing To Discover What You Think

Let us postulate that we have been grappling, mentally and orally, with a pending significant decision. As the body of information grows, it may be useful to begin to record it in writing. The decision-making format outlined earlier is useful for that purpose, and also enables one to further the process by recording the information under the appropriate headings of facts, disputed assertions of facts, assumptions, hypotheses, potential options, and so forth.

It is a truism that an inquiry and the written record of it grow as time and effort accumulate. In addition, and perhaps more importantly, writing clarifies thinking. It forces us to compose, and in the process to question whether we have accurately recorded the available information and our views regarding it. The spoken and written languages are, in effect, two different languages, using the same or similar words by conveying a different import of them. Neither is a perfect means of expressing meaning precisely: each has some advantages over the other. Speech is more economic, usable second by second or minute by minute to express thoughts as they emerge, ordinarily adequate to the purpose of the moment and situation, requiring some thought but issuing spontaneously. In direct speech, where the speaker is visible to the listener, it has the added advantage of the speaker's manner and body language. It is the more economical means because it engages minds in dialogue, allowing rapid exchange of ideas, the mutual stimulus of ideas, and adjustments accordingly. Most of the everyday decisions of personal and occupational life can and should be addressed through the spoken word.

On the other hand, rapidity implies lack of time for reflection and clarification. Conversation is often a necessary path to determining the need for a more formal approach. A time comes, therefore, when one may wish to back off, to consider one's views, to write them out as one's considered position. It is for this reason that we call for position papers on important matters under consideration. The written word carries more weight precisely because it requires us to question the factuality and significance of the information we are using, to recognize and state what we must assume for lack of verifiable information, to examine our views, to clarify them and state them more precisely, to add all the necessary modifiers and caveats. In going through that process, we are forced to examine our own established viewpoints and thoughts critically, and to develop a more precise statement of them. At the end of such a writing exercise, one may ask: "Is this what I really think? Would I sign this paper as a formal statement of my position if the paper was prepared by some else?" If one cay say "Yes" to these questions, the writing has accomplished its purpose.

It's Not Easy Being Rational

The central theme of this discussion has been that humans should manage their personal lives, their occupations, and their institutions on the basis of reason appropriately blended with emotion: with "bounded rationality," in Herbert Simon's very apt term.

Further, to reach agreement or to advance knowledge, humans must employ "bounded rationality" in cooperative dialogue. Much of humanity does not think or operate in the suggested manner, partially because we humans already have stored in memory a number of beliefs that shape decisions. A large part of the non-Western world suppresses rational dialogue in favor of religious or political fervor. The Western world is not immune to this phenomenon: some influential individuals and institutions in it also seek to suppress free inquiry and free speech by imposing "political correctness," "speech codes," and similar measures upon society at large. This is an old problem assuming new forms, permeating Western world universities, governments, businesses, information media, and other institutions and demanding compliance or silence. It is, as it historically has been, a drag on progress, because it forces people to be constantly cautious, and thus to think more about avoiding conflict than about improving what exists or creating something new. Some of the fixed beliefs held by members of our own Western society, and the sets of fixed beliefs that define other societies, are major boundaries to rationality. They turn questions of fact into matters of opinion or faith, moving the matter from the realm of rational argumentation and fact-finding to a contest between good (us) and evil (them). Approaching any matter from this standpoint relieves the advocates of the obligation to defend their position.

Freedom of thought and expression is not simply a political principle embodied in the First Amendment to the Constitution of the United States. Properly used, it is the instrument of progress and adaptation to change. The five or six-thousand-years record of human history informs us that human progress is not inevitable, that our present government, public institutions, industrial and scientific strength, and wealth owe their existence to the freedom to think and innovate. That contemporary freedom is, in historical terms, a phenomenon of the reawakening of thought and inquiry in the Western world during the last four centuries. The history of those centuries demonstrates that societies, institutions, commercial enterprises, and individuals that allow and encourage freedom of thought and of speech adapt to change, or produce change, and therefore prosper. Those that fail to embrace freedom of thought and expression can be and have been surpassed in every measure of progress by those that do. Moslem fundamentalism, a significant force within and outside Islam, asserts that the Koran provides all necessary human knowledge. It therefore teaches and practices little else, and treats as infidels and enemies those who do not accept its beliefs. It has severely retarded progress in the Islamic world, and continues to present a threat to all human freedom and advancement. To extremists among such people, it is rational to kill those who do not accept their beliefs and to destroy their institutions. No informal logic dialogue is possible with them, because the conflict opposes deadly conviction against the right to think.

In our own Western culture, in both external and internal affairs, examples of common errors and logical fallacies, of hasty or tardy decisions, of intrusion of "The box" of fixed beliefs and raw emotions into questions that demand rational processes, are commonplace. Thinkers who advocate significant change or venture outside "the political correctness Box" are likely to encounter immediate resistance, very often from within the very institutions that were traditional defenders of freedom of thought and expression. On the other hand, if the proposal is immediately perceived as useful, it will have many claimants to its origination.

It's not easy being rational.

Chapter 5

Sources of Error

THE THINKING REED

Wise Man or Woman (Sometimes)

How can it be that mankind, the species *homo sapiens*, "wise man" or "intelligent man," "wise woman" or "intelligent woman," can also make decisions that can be seen in retrospect as mistaken, or at odds with external reality, or - stupid? I have earlier addressed some aspects of that question, from the standpoint of method. Here I begin to focus more sharply on the individual human decision-maker.

A broad answer to the question lies in the complex nature of *homo sapiens*. From one aspect, *homo sapiens* deserves Shakespeare's accolade: "What a piece of work is a man! how noble in reason! how infinite in faculty! . . . in form and moving, how express and admirable! in action how like an angel! in apprehension how like a god! the beauty of the world! the paragon of animals!"[13] This praise fits those men and women who have created and passed on knowledge, employed nature to serve human ends, created vast cities and great machines and civilized societies, produced great art and literature. They can indeed be called "the paragon of animals," for no species has so changed the world and itself.

Unfortunately, *homo sapiens* has other dimensions: his works have included much that is anything but noble in reason, or infinite in faculty, or godlike in apprehension, or noteworthy for beauty. In Blaise Pascal's classic phrase, "Man is but a reed, the weakest in nature, but he is a thinking reed." The Latin name *homo sapiens* is somewhat contradicted by a Latin phrase describing one of *homo sapiens*' characteristics: *humanum est errare*, or "to err is human." If we can agree - as we readily should - that there are some things in the human psyche that prominently lead to mistakes, we must then seek out those qualities and try to find ways to reduce their effect. We begin by looking at *homo sapiens* in his/her moments as a rational decision-maker,

I have asserted that lack of a **process** or failure to follow it, and failure to have a **decision-making mode** and to transition to it, are prominent sources of error. I have also recognized that it is difficult to conceive of a decision making situation devoid of emotional content, and repeatedly emphasized the conflict raised within us at the meeting points of reason and emotion. Mankind has long recognized the need for balance between the two, and the frequent difficulty of determining where that balance should lie. I am seeking here to cast some useful light on the problems of attaining and holding that balance.

The enormous role of the emotions in human decision making is illustrated by the fact that they provide the locus of most major works of literature and the performing arts. Emotion is not devoid of reason: it has a certain element of intelligence on its own. Anger, an emotion ordinarily and properly viewed as a dangerously negative influence, can be an appropriate influence when justifiably aroused and properly controlled and directed. Fear produces the fight-or-run reaction that is essential to self-preservation. Love in its concrete sense - to love and to be loved - is resoundingly viewed and sought after as essential to a healthy and happy life. On its negative side,

Shakespeare's Hamlet, in his famous "To be or not to be" soliloquy, speaks of the "pangs of despised love" as one of life's afflictions, and love is notoriously said to be blind. Other "good" emotions - such as pity, sympathy, charity, generosity, trust - can obscure rational assessment of whether they are justified by the facts or should dominate the decision process. Transactions based on trust can produce serious monetary and emotional losses, particularly if an act such as paying in advance or entrusting another with something one values is given in exchange for a promise that cannot be monitored and enforced. It bears repeating, then, that the problem is to find that middle ground between two parts of ourselves, to be neither the slave of our emotional self nor of our rational self.

Allow a word of caution here. Although we speak of *homo sapiens* in terms of characteristics shared by all humans, one must continue to hold in mind that humans live within a number of cultures, that different cultures impart different modes of thought and world-views, and consequently generate different intellectual and emotional responses to the same set of facts, or even responses that deny the facts. What would be accepted as rational or acceptable behavior in one culture might be viewed differently in another. The reader should be constantly aware that this work is done within the context of that vaguely bounded reality, our own Western culture. Some judgments may be valid only for our own culture, others for humans in general.

This returns us to an earlier comment: we humans bring to the decision-making occasion all the mental and intellectual and emotional baggage we have accumulated in a lifetime of childhood and adult indoctrination, experience, education, and assimilation of beliefs and habits characteristic of our cultural milieu. We seem also to bring certain implicit assumptions: that the current "state of nature" will essentially continue, that the future will be essentially like the past, that change will occur at a pace we can accommodate.

In particular, we appear to be reluctant to contemplate the probability of disastrous events. I return to an earlier reference to the beginnings of World War II. Roberta Wohlstetter, in her massive study of America's Pearl Harbor blunder, comments on one of the threads of causation that allowed the Japanese to achieve surprise: "Apparently human beings have a stubborn attachment to old beliefs and an equally stubborn resistance to new material that will upset . . . [the old beliefs]."[14] While not specifically informed that the Japanese would attack Pearl Harbor, the local commanders had sufficient information to conclude that a Japanese attack somewhere was definitely possible or probable. So, why not an attack on Pearl Harbor, the home port of most of the American Pacific Fleet and in other respects a major American military base? A brief answer, summarizing Wohlstetter's heavily detailed account: *because the new information was not sufficiently conclusive to penetrate the shield surrounding the existing beliefs.* The Japanese military leadership, for its part, is said to have decided for war in the belief that striking a heavy military blow in the beginning and overrunning a huge area of the Pacific and Asia would present the United States with a military problem of such magnitude that the United States would not make the effort and sacrifice necessary to overcome it. In actuality, the attack had the effect said to have been expressed by Japanese Admiral Isoroku Yamamoto immediately thereafter: "I fear we have awakened a sleeping giant and filled him with a terrible purpose." Other realms of human affairs reinforce the hypothesis that *homo sapiens* does not wish to address the possibility of a disastrous event. This is the "Medusa head" phenomenon, drawn from the early Greek mythology: if one looked directly at the serpent-haired Medusa, one immediately turned to stone. Joseph Stalin received repeated and clear warnings of German preparations to attack the Soviet Union, from both his own intelligence sources and Great Britain, but authorized only minimal and disastrously inadequate preparatory measures. Still earlier, and as earlier noted, British Prime Minister Neville Chamberlain, unwilling to face the "Medusa head" prospect of another war with Germany, adopted the policy of "appeasement" of Hitler and Germany, believing that he could essentially buy off Hitler by measures that could only make Hitler, and Germany, stronger and Britain's potential allies weaker. The opposite effects were clearly more likely, and in fact the policy did increase Hitler's political and military power, his self-assurance, and his personal and national ambitions. It was an important step toward World War II. Information developed after World War II disclosed the strong probability that a firm stand by Britain and France would have resulted in the German Army removing Hitler from power.

Turning to business decisions, there is much anecdotal evidence that the managers of weakened commercial enterprises resist the conclusion that the enterprise is likely to fail, and managers therefore do not take the early steps necessary to avoid ultimate liquidation. In the realm of personal decision-making, in spite of warnings some persons residing in the projected paths of hurricanes stay in place in the belief that "it will go somewhere else" or "we can ride it out." They do not assess the level of probability that it may not "go somewhere else," or that if they do "ride it out," food, water, gasoline, health care, sanitation, electric power, communications, transportation, and other ordinary services will not be available for an extended period. Over a considerable period of years, political leaders of Louisiana and New Orleans neglected necessary maintenance and updating of levees and pumping systems, then delayed issuance of mandatory evacuations and other preparatory measures for the disastrous 2005 Hurricane Katrina until too late and failed to protect the transport that might have facilitated evacuation of survivors. Investors disregarded clear warning signals that the 1990's "bubble" in the price of technology stocks could not be sustained, that the "housing bubble" that followed it in the early 2000's was similarly unsustainable, that the collapse of the housing marker would lead to the collapse of financial markets, that the 1929 stock market crash was likely, and that the much earlier "South Seas Bubble" and the frenzied Tulip Craze must also collapse.

These phenomena suggest that, if the "rational" decision requires us to adjust our strongly held beliefs or our life style, we tend to "screen out" information that would require major adjustments or changes in what we already believe or require us to confront threatening possibilities. "Screening" of incoming information, if defined as assuring that the information is substantially true and relevant, is clearly necessary for the reasons earlier stated. I employ the word "screening" here in the sense of refusing to accept information that contradicts what we already believe. Socrates made the case a few thousand years ago, and subsequent philosophers and events have affirmed it, that much of what we already believe is also not demonstrably true by generally accepted standards of factuality or tests of truth, or not necessarily unaffected by changes in "states of nature." Philosophers engaged in the study of knowledge have warned us repeatedly: belief is not knowledge.

So, we carry within ourselves a set of beliefs and traits that we are reluctant to part with, but by definition our decision-making mode may require major changes in some of them. The transition to **Decision Making Mode** may be compared to entering a room. It is neither possible to leave a part of one's physical self outside the room nor to leave behind one's existing beliefs, which include one's self-perception, outside the decision-making mode. Similarly, we cannot leave behind our emotional self. Moreover, there are surely times when our emotions may offer the better choice. As in art, which reflects life, we must allow our emotions into our decision making mode. But, it is feasible to emphasize or de-emphasize certain aspects of one's persona, to be conscious of one's beliefs and emotional attachment to them, to have sufficient humility to absorb new information and weigh it on its merits. The decision-making mode will then leave open the finding that one's beliefs may require adjustment in the light of new information or new situations, and/ or that one's emotions require some taming.

The following passages explore some ways that may help us strike that desired balance between our rational and emotional selves. We begin with a convenient, established paradigm: the "Seven Deadly Sins." They have earned that classification because they have long been most prominently identified with behavior in which the emotions have taken control, and three of them are linked to disastrously bad decisions.

The Thinking Reed and the Seven Deadly Sins

In alphabetical order, the seven are anger, envy, gluttony, greed, lust, pride, and sloth. They were grouped together in writings as early as the sixth century, and may have been a fixture of earlier thought. Early Christian-era philosophical and religious thought perceived them as "deadly" because they ran counter to the moral virtues and led to other "sins." More recent opinion perceives them as "deadly" because they abandon good judgment in favor of satisfaction of the ego or the concupiscent appetites, the so-called "pleasures of the flesh." The seven deadly sins are things of the emotions, excesses that can overwhelm the rational self. They are as much a part of man as the rational and contemplative, and too often more powerful. The earlier Christian-era treatment included an approximate ranking of their seriousness: vainglory (excessive pride), covetousness (classified as excessive desire for fortune, fame, glory, or other forms of self-gratification), lust (perceived as excessive or illicit sexual desire), envy, gluttony (including excessive use of alcohol), anger, sloth. One can readily agree that all are to be avoided, but some have been and remain conspicuous for their negative effect on decisions. We first visit the three of those afflictions that are most frequently encountered, inter-connected, and arguably most damaging: vainglorious pride (hubris), anger, and inordinate covetousness.

Pride, or Hubris? Pride in one's work, in one's integrity, in one's achievements, in one's skills, even in one's appearance, are appropriate individual emotions. Moreover, achievement feeds on recognition, is nourished and reinforced by it. Recognitions of achievement ranging from the highest international and national levels down to the lowest level of employee and student provide psychic income. Non-monetary forms of recognition are often valued much more than money, and are essential to encourage effort and excellence at all levels of society and human organizations. Justifiable pride is necessary to self-confidence, which is reinforced by positive recognition. Self-confidence is in turn indispensable to decision-making in careers and life, and those who occupy high places in human affairs must also have the high confidence necessary to their decision making duties. One must therefore have high respect and regard for achievement and a corresponding level of pride.

The level of pride we are addressing here is out of balance with genuine achievement and ability: it is inordinate self-adulation, *hubris*. Hubris is defined as "exaggerated pride or self-confidence, often resulting in retribution." It is a form of self-delusion, a level of self-regard and a sense of one's own competence or level of achievement beyond that of other persons that actuality does not warrant. No one is immune to it. It may afflict some who have little basis for it, but it is perhaps the most common affliction of recognizable success. It therefore disproportionately affects persons whose decisions may have great influence on society, government, or economic affairs. For that reason, it is important because it not only endangers the careers and lives of persons to whom society has entrusted much, but also those affected by their decisions.

Hubris influences decision-making adversely in the following ways. The victim, hereinafter identified for convenience as "The Great One," perceives an opinion contrary to his own as a challenge to his greatness, and rejects it, often scornfully. The holder of the differing opinion, particularly if he is The Great One's subordinate, and his peers who have witnessed one or more of these exhibitions of what Shakespeare aptly termed "the proud man's contumely," then elect to avoid humiliation, futility, and damage to their career prospects. They cease to offer views which are known to differ with those of The Great One, they avoid venturing into areas where The Great One's views are not known, and consequently they do not offer creative ideas. Some will seek employment elsewhere, particularly with organizations more open to creative ideas. Some will continue to press their views, and find that they are sidelined or no longer employed by that particular organization. In every case, vital upward communication is cut off, thinking subordinates are lost, and those who remain have been administered an object lesson in the penalties for differing with The Great One. It is, of course, entirely possible that The Great One's views are well founded, the subordinate's views less so, but the subordinate's humiliation nevertheless has harmed the organization's communication channels, and thus its decision-making capability. The Great One has placed an invisible wall of ego between himself and the flow of information and opinion vital to the decision-making process. The organization's nervous system has been crippled or deformed. The process of creative destruction, so vital to adapting the organization to real and anticipated change, has been slowed or terminated.

A variant of this process occurs when The Great One perceives himself as guardian of the organization's culture, or that of a particular profession within it. For example, the manager who is also an engineer (or lawyer or accountant, etc.), and proud of it to the extent that he scorns the views of other professions represented among his subordinates and peers, will soon get, at best, a trickle of information from those professions, and none of it volunteered.

We have noted earlier and repeatedly that the survival and well-being of an organism or organization is a function of its adaptation to changed conditions. Hubris can penetrate and become widespread in an organization. Organizational success may produce inflated organizational pride. If most people in an organization believe it is already "the best," the incentive to improve may be dulled. Excessive pride stifles the process of recognizing that a different "state of nature" is evolving or has already evolved, and hence delays or defeats adaptation to that change. It can blind an organization to the threats from without and the weaknesses within. For meaningful examples, consider the transient dominance of certain companies in the computer and communications industries.

Hubris afflicts families as well as organizations. The proud, dictatorial, "don't dare to disagree with me" style shuts down communication and discussion, suppresses family members' aspirations, allows perceived slights to fester, and may destroy family cohesion. The junior members of the family, and all those affected by the family tyrant's role, will opt out either openly or simply seek a "damage-limiting" strategy: as little exposure as possible.

Hubris is also a destroyer of those afflicted by it. Recall that hubris is defined as "exaggerated pride or self-confidence, often resulting in retribution." Excessive pride may also inject in the male "Great One" a sense of "machismo," defined as "exaggerated pride in a masculinity, often accompanied by a minimal sense of responsibility and disregard of consequences." That phenomenon, "a minimal sense of responsibility and disregard of consequences," has occupied a large place in the annals of mankind. "Pride goeth before destruction, and a haughty spirit before a fall," says the Christian bible at *Proverbs* 16:18.

Sophocles, some twenty-four hundred years or more ago, wrote:

> The tyrant is a child of Pride
> Who drinks from his great sickening cup
> Recklessness and vanity,
> Until from his high crest headlong
> He plummets to the dust of hope. [3]

In one of the most conspicuous examples in literary fiction based on fact, Shakespeare's Cardinal Wolsey laments his dismissal (from his position as essentially the British Prime Minister), together with forfeit of all possessions, by King Henry VIII:

> . . . . . . "I have ventured
> Like little wanton boys that swim on bladders,
> This many summers on a sea of glory,
> But far beyond my depth: my high-blown
>   pride
> At length broke under me and now has left me,
> Weary and old with service, to the mercy
> Of a rude stream, that must forever hide me. [4]

Alexander Pope characterized pride in the following terms:

> Of all the causes that conspire to blind,
> Man's erring judgment, and misguide
>   the mind,

> What the weak head with strongest
> bias rules,
> Is pride, the never-failing vice of fools.[5]

These excerpts, samplings from the whole panoply of human life, suggest the dangers hubris produces for ourselves. In both sexes, hubris may lead to a sense of immunity, of being beyond the laws and norms of conduct of lesser (ordinary) persons. Deceptions and self-deceptions are engaged in, imprudent risks are run, colleagues and friends are lost. Although some Great Ones carry their burden of conceit to the grave, the day of retribution comes for some others, as it did with the real and fictional Wolsey and more recently corporate executives who have engaged, among other criminal activities, in "creative accounting," otherwise known as "cooking the books." A self-described "really Star CEO" is hired to head a major corporation in difficulty, introduces "a creative accounting" to give the perception of success, is found out, dismissed in shame, and left forever an unemployable pariah. Others (e. g., Tyco International, Enron, WorldCom executives) are found guilty of a variety of crimes, sentenced to various punishments, required to surrender their illicit wealth, and sentenced to prison terms. Consider the parallel with Cardinal Wolsey's lament "when he falls, he falls like Lucifer, Never to hope again."[6]

Pride, as we have here defined it, is often accompanied by a tendency to anger easily, to take offense at any apparent lack of appreciation of The Great One's greatness, to disagree angrily and summarily. Greed and covetousness enter, in the sense that The Great One demands more honors, more wealth, more fame, more advancement, more distinctions that separate him from what he now regards as the common herd of lesser persons.

Hubris - excessive pride - is, then, deplorable and harmful to both The Great One, to his subordinates and others around him, to his decision making capacity, and to other aspects of his responsibilities. But, like any excess, hubris has its opposite: a lack of self-confidence or a sense of inadequacy that translates into procrastination, delay, and shrinking from the necessity to face or seek out a decision-making situation. As noted above, self-confidence, willingness to identify and confront difficult problems and situations, is an essential personality trait of managers and of all who face life head-on. Good decisions are more likely to emerge from those who seek, find, and maintain the desirable balance between excessive pride and excessive modesty.

Anger. Anger is not necessarily or entirely negative. Life poses situations and circumstances that ought to anger us, and do. But anger that surges uncontrolled ordinarily contributes nothing to the rational and much to the urge to act, to lash out wildly, to blame others. Anger begets anger in others because its expression is abusive and threatening. From that point angry parties often engage in conflict behavior which not only does not resolve the matter but moves it to a higher emotional intensity, "resort to ineffectual behavior" in the context of psychology, and a more difficult situation. As this level of anger dissipates, it is often replaced by regret, shame, contrition, and a more rational search to correct not only the initial fault but also the situation (the new "state of nature") that anger has created.

Controlled anger, on the other hand, informs others of our determination to act upon a perceived offense or error, and allows us to switch to decision-making mode, to blend anger with deliberation in a manner conducive to constructive action. The rise of anger within ourselves should, then, immediately trigger recognition of the need to bring the emotional and the rational into balance, to turn on the decision making mode switch.

For some managers, constantly being or appearing to be somewhat angry constitutes the essence of their management style. Some may be genuinely unhappy, perhaps justly so. Those afflicted with inordinate hubris may also be, or appear to be, continuously angry or prone to anger. Others adopt the appearance as part of their persona, apparently on the implicit assumption that it projects firmness or toughness and a demanding attitude, "machismo," and thus motivates subordinates through fear. In either case, anger or the appearance of anger is the enemy of rational decision making. It infects both the angry person's decision making and that of subordinates and colleagues. It creates and maintains an atmosphere of tension that constrains communication, initiative, and creativity. The circumstances under which this might be an effective management style perhaps exist, but it is certainly not suited to situations in which subordinates are at liberty to seek other managers or other employers.

A parallel observation applies to persons committed to a particular public policy objective, often regarded as a "cause." As we earlier observed, every major decision involves both probable desired consequences and probable undesired consequences. Advocates of particular causes stress the desired consequences without the due diligence and comparison with the undesired consequences that a rational process demands. At its extreme, advocates may become imbued with a sense of moral superiority, anger at their opposition, with an accompanying perception of themselves as opposing the "forces of evil." This attitude lays claim to both the moral and intellectual high ground. The advocates' view is encapsulated in the slogan, "We're mad as hell, and we aren't going to take it any more." Since they cannot or do not make their case persuasively by rational argumentation, they resort to demonstrations, "hue and cry" tactics, appeals to fear, and portrayal of the opposition as evil or ignorant, or both. The contemporary discords over "global warning" and its causes, drilling in the Arctic National Wildlife Refuge (ANWR), globalism, anti-terrorism, American intervention in the Middle East, Islam versus "infidels," American and European differences of opinion, and various other issues provide ample examples. Rational argumentation is sidelined: the decision process becomes an angry conflict waged for a political or public opinion majority or for a personal, verbal triumph.

A further comment regarding anger: the field of psychology informs us that each of us has a "threshold of irascibility." If our particular threshold is low, we anger quickly; if high, we are less prone to anger. It seems, then, that the person seeking to become a better decision-maker should try consciously to set that threshold at a "slow to anger" level, and consciously prepare to recognize the onset of anger as the point **to switch into decision-making mode**. Moreover, our "threshold of irascibility" is not fixed: frustration, disappointments, poor health, stress, fatigue, and other unpleasantries lower the threshold. The good things of life raise it. The enjoyment of life, a good in itself, is thus conducive to good decisions. But, as suggested immediately below, there can be excessive desire for valued things in life.

Greed, or covetousness. An oft repeated quote from Robert Browning asserts that a man's "reach should exceed his grasp." If taken to mean that one's ends should be always beyond one's means, that is a formula for lifelong discontent. If taken to mean that one should continuously aspire to greater competence, greater achievement, greater character, it is a formula for continuous self-improvement and the satisfaction that comes from it. Of course, people who have followed the latter course rightfully expect recognition and advancement. There is thus an indistinct border, which one must find for one's self, between laudable and self-satisfying ambition and dishonorable and unfulfilling greed.

Hubris and greed may propel their victim over that indistinct border. Hubris demands nourishment. When desire becomes greed - for adulation, advancement, fame, wealth, recognition of greatness, or what one wills - and goes unfulfilled, anger may result. An inordinately proud, unfulfilled, and angry person is not likely to produce good decisions.

Envy, Gluttony, Lust, Sloth. These comprise the remainder of the deadly seven. While each represents a large subject, it will suffice here that we recognize their presence and their effects, in ourselves or others. Envy motivates us to equal or outdo others in some manner, and possibly to disparage the achievements of others. It proceeds from a mistaken assumption regarding the problem, and violates the standard that a decision option be feasible, practicable, legal, moral, ethical, and reasonable. In his classic Julius Caesar, Shakespeare depicted envy as the motivation of the plotters, excepting Brutus, for the assassination of Caesar. The ambitious plotter Cassius, seeking Caesar's power, addresses Brutus to turn him against Caesar:

> Why, man, he doth bestride the narrow world
> Like a Colossus, and we petty men
> Walk under his legs and peep about
> To find ourselves dishonorable graves.
> Men at some time are masters of their fates:
> The fault, dear Brutus, is not in our stars,
> But in ourselves, that we are underlings.
> Brutus and Caesar, what should be in that
> 'Caesar'?
> Why should that name be sounded more than
> yours?
> Upon what meat does this our Caesar feed,
> That he has grown so great? [7]

Gluttony , which may take the form of excessive appetite for food, drink, sex, honors, homage, and other pleasures of the body and mind, poses obvious consequences and risks. Lust, which can of course lead to rich and rewarding experiences, can and does result in disasters if one fails to recognize that it can lead to undesired and unforeseen consequences. Sloth, in decision-making context, is one source of the "satisficer" approach, the failure to identify and weigh all the reasonable options, to perform the required "due diligence." Its adverse effect on other aspects of human life are important but well and widely understood.

The Other Emotions

It may well be that the "seven deadly sins" account for a disproportionate share of the seriously bad decisions that overwhelming emotions engender. If so, our visit with them may have been proportionate to their role. Other emotions, too numerous to address separately, are generally regarded as neither sins nor deadly, ordinarily have desirable effects upon our decision-making, and are well-regarded. Love, sympathy, pity, charity, kindness are regarded as positive qualities, as indeed they are in most cases. But, as we have previously observed, love can blind one to reality. Appeals to pity and charity, coupled with excessive trust by the recipient, can lead us to open our hearts and purses without verification of the need. It is said that "man wills the good." Our desire to do good can lead to acceptance of fallacious appeals, another source of error to which I now turn.

The Notorious Fallacies

The so-called "logical fallacies" have a long history in human affairs, and continue to appear in every form of communication and dialogue. The fact that they have played an important and essentially negative role in the human search for knowledge is illustrated by the attention given them as early as the early Greek and Roman civilizations, and perhaps much earlier. They have been categorized and given Latin names, to make them recognizable wherever and in what form or language they may appear. They remain in use in part because their user may not realize that his proposition is fallacious, or perhaps even more often because he knows it is and regards it as an effective tool. The concept of a cooperative effort to reach a logical conclusion is perhaps the farthest thought from the minds of many who are simply advocates. A substantial school of thought holds that the use of fallacies and other odious techniques is a powerful and legitimate way to "win an argument." The philosopher Arthur Schopenhauer's *The Art of Controversy* lists thirty-eight ways, of which some are fallacies and all are morally indefensible, to that end: winning.

Just as one should avoid bad information, one should learn to recognize and avoid the logical fallacies in argumentation, as well as others that are fallacies but perhaps undeserving of the title "logical." They are important to anyone who seeks a cooperative dialogue to reach understanding, both to avoid using them inadvertently in their own reasoning and to recognize and call attention to them when they are used by others.

A fallacy as used herein refers to an error in reasoning or a mistaken or weak argument in support of a proposition or statement. I include, in those broad categories, deliberate attempts to mislead or persuade by altering, embellishing, downplaying, or concealing facts, and employing emotional appeals to obscure the facts. Thus, we are again dealing with a large and serious matter that has its own extensive literature. The subject is too large, the fallacies too numerous to list and explore exhaustively here, but a few of them may account for a disproportionate share of reasoning errors. Those few must be mentioned, starting with fallacies applying to causation.

A frequently encountered fallacy involves the occurrence of two events, either consecutively or concurrently, and the fallacy of inferring that one is the cause of the other. The Latin names for these two are aptly descriptive: *post hoc, ergo propter hoc* (after the event, therefore because of the event) and *cum hoc, ergo propter hoc* (with the event, therefore because of the event). In fact, sequential or concurrent occurrence of two events merely suggest some degree of probability of connection. The possibilities are: one indeed caused the other; they had a single common cause; they had unrelated separate causes; one of the events was only one of many causes of the other; one may have been adverse to the occurrence of the other. The important fact to store here is the time-worn but often disregarded caveat: "correlation does not establish causation." It may provide a good place to begin the search for cause, but it should not be taken as sufficient without further investigation and conclusive proof.

Fallacies of appeal to the emotions are prevalent in our contemporary society, too numerous to list. They appeal to pity, sympathy, the threat of adverse consequences, moral goodness, sense of obligation, political orientation, sexuality, vanity, self-indulgence, and a host of others.

The *ad populem* fallacy appeals to the emotions by asserting that a proposition is true because it is widely believed. It is often combined with appeal to authority, e. g., "most scientists now believe," followed by a declaration of what "most scientists" are alleged to believe. The first problem with such claims is the absence of conclusive evidence of its truth: how was it determined that "most scientists believe?" Second, how strongly held are their beliefs, and why? A further problem lies in whether what most people in any particular profession believe on a question outside their field of inquiry - and often, within both their field and their scope of inquiry - is conclusive evidence of truth. Scientists and other professionals are spread across many disciplines, with the pursuit of each a demanding activity that limits opportunity not only to remain abreast of other disciplines, but also to remain abreast of everything in their own field. The history of scientific thought and discovery gives credence to the view that, within a specific scientific discipline, scientific "knowledge" should be viewed as tentative, as the current hypothesis or "paradigm." Virtually all appeals to authority exclude dissenting authorities. Conclusion: all appeals to accept a proposition because it is popular or is held by any group require critical examination One must ask a question that goes back to the Romans, and probably to the beginnings of human society: "Qui bono?" Who benefits? The so-called authority may in fact lack the required credentials, or the specific knowledge, or the integrity to be authoritative. The respected, knowledgeable, and conscientious authority can also simply be mistaken.

The *argumentum ad ignorantiam* (argument to ignorance) holds that something is true because it has not been proved to be false. A familiar contemporary example is the proposition that many sightings of "unidentified flying objects" are of spacecraft from another planet visiting the earth, believed by many people on the basis that it has not been disproved. Another proposition holds that "global warming" is due to human activity in the last few centuries. The critical thinker might hold that either or both of these propositions have a probability greater that zero of being correct: the true believer might hold that either or both are correct because they have not been disproved. The latter position amounts, at best, to a weak argument. The *argumentum ad ignorantiam* does, however, have legitimate uses. For example, the prudent person would presume all guns loaded, all snakes poisonous or otherwise dangerous, all investments involving risk, pending proof to the contrary. In a different version of prudence and fairness, our system of criminal justice presumes that a person charged with a crime is innocent until proved guilty beyond reasonable doubt.

The *slippery slope* argument holds that adoption of a particular position or policy will lead to a series of adverse consequences, without establishing the probability of all or any of the suggested adverse consequences occurring, and without examining the probability of desired consequences. The *strawman* fallacy (not to be confused with the "strawman" draft document used as a locus for discussion) attempts to refute a proposition by recasting it in a grotesque or extreme manner; in other words, by refuting a proposition that has not been advocated. The *tu quoque* fallacy attempts to defend a mistaken or weak argument by alleging that the opposition has made the same or a similar mistake. The *ad hominem* fallacy (argument against the person) attacks the motives or character of the opposition person or persons, shifting the ground from the merits of the proposition to the merits of those advocating it. *Ad hominem* arguments do, however, have a place when the problem involves a person's credentials, character, or qualifications. The *false dilemma* argues that only two options exist, although there may be more. The *false analogy* compares two or more events or situations as being alike although they are in fact dissimilar or the similarity cannot be established. A common form of the false analogy is "we tried that before and it didn't work." This argument can be valid only if precisely the same attempt was made under precisely the same conditions. The *hasty generalization* argues for adoption of an inductive generalization that is insufficiently supported. The *exclusion fallacy*, as its name implies, excludes evidence that might support a different conclusion. The inappropriately named *begging the question* fallacy establishes premises (presumes facts not in evidence) in the statement of the question or problem that determine the conclusion. The familiar example is the "when are you going to stop beating your wife?" question. (Refer to the earlier observations on the importance of getting the problem or question statement right). The *slothful induction* fallacy denies the logical conclusion of a strong inductive argument. It is an element of the phenomenon of resistance to change and adaptation.

The *affirming the consequent* fallacy lies at an opposite pole, in too readily accepting an apparently logical argument. It reverses the logical statement "If P, then Q" to "Q, therefore P." This fallacy arises in the use of hypotheses, whose utility is cited elsewhere herein, in reaching conclusions as to the validity of a statement or proposition. A familiar example is the hypothesis that if the sun revolved around a non-rotating earth, then there would be consistent and predictable periods of darkness and sunlight upon places on the earth. Since the latter proposition is easily affirmed by daily observation, the actual fact, equally consistent with daily observation, that a rotating and tilted earth revolved around the sun was long obscured and, when it surfaced, much disputed.

There are, of course, many more identified fallacies than this brief work can address. They deserve much more attention in the course of one's acquaintance with sources of error, but the preceding discussion should serve as a warning that disinformation, misinformation, and outright falsehood can be and often are packaged into an apparently logical discussion. Critical thinking is an effective antidote to these perils.

We should not leave the subject of fallacies without identifying a few additional sources of error, although they do not fit precisely under the rubric of logical fallacies.

Method as a Source of Error

Sophistry is a method that packages confusing, insincere, fallacious arguments in a cloak of logic. Although sophistry arose as
a school of thought and teaching among the early Greek philosophers, in modern usage it refers to the practice of appealing to the
preferences, prejudices, and emotions of decision-makers, without
regard to the truth or validity of the sophists' argument. The soph-
ist would argue that the actual truth or validity of an argument is
extraneous: the only important feature is the ruling of the decision
maker or makers, and the ruling of the decision makers is equivalent to established truth. Sophistry is widely employed in legal
proceedings, debate, public relations, advertising, and other forms
of advocacy. At its worst, it is deception, employing logical fallacies, part-truths and downright falsehoods, appeals to the emotions
and prejudices, irresponsible innuendo, trivial criticisms, and other
scurrilous methods, to influence audiences. Its widespread use un-
derlines the need for alertness and critical thinking.

Casuistry refers to decision-making by applying religious doctrine, or ethical principles, or political doctrine, or simply what
one already believes, to bound and shape the decision. The political
"isms" such as socialism, liberalism, conservatism, and others, when
used as the guideline for decisions with respect to any matter, government or private, represent examples of casuistry. In one of its
variants, casuistry is related to sophistry in that it can be used to in-
tentionally mislead or support a weak argument. It is essentially a
method of arguing from some selected base point that is accepted as
valid: a so-called "paradigm." A familiar example is the use of case
law or some principle of morality or ethics or political doctrine in
an attempt to decide a particular matter. The circumstances of the
matter being addressed are then compared to the paradigm. Casuistry would hold that, if the circumstances are similar, the matter

should be decided in the manner of the paradigm: if dissimilar, it should be decided differently. The opportunities to mislead or to support a weak argument, or to reach a decision without critical examination, are evident, and casuistry has developed a deserved reputation for being both immoral and an effective method of using false analogies. On the other hand, proceeding by comparison with an established principle or truth, and judging how well the circumstances of a particular matter conform to that standard, can be a very useful and logical approach. A familiar example is the use of a data base of criminal method *(modus operandi)* to identify possible suspects in criminal investigations. If the manner of performing a crime is similar to the manner most often used by a known criminal, that person may be reasonably considered a suspect. "Profiling" is a similar example, as is, in medical practice, the use of symptoms in diagnosing disease. Casuistry, properly used, can be a legitimate and powerful decision-making tool.

Thinking Inside the Box

Now permit the resurfacing of a matter, earlier associated with the Pearl Harbor surprise, that I will term, for convenience, the "fallacy of the status quo." It is a mind set that confines the thinking of individuals and organizations. It assumes that the current "state of nature" will prevail indefinitely, and it therefore fails to provide the necessary basis for adapting to change. The reader will recognize this fallacy in frequently heard sentiments such as "Everything's O. K.," or "we are already the best (country, company, product, armed force, military unit, organization)," or "we have most of the business," or "that isn't in our business plan," or "you can't believe that XYZ (corporation, country, person) is a serious competitor," or any of a number of similar expressions that amount to excessively optimistic implicit assumptions regarding future prospects. It is reported that then General Motors Chief Executive Officer Roger Smith, when asked in the 1980's how GM planned to compete with low cost European and Asian imports, replied "Why, our answer to that is a two-year-old Buick."

The phenomenon also applies to individual humans, who may not see threats to some important elements of their lives. I do not suggest that any individual or organization should exist in a state of continuous anxiety or paranoia, but one can point to any number of cases in which the mighty have fallen because conditions changed faster then they changed or they failed to perceive the threat. In the 1960's and 1970's, the IBM Corporation had achieved a position of industry predominance based upon business practices and products that would soon be outmoded. The failure to foresee and adapt to rapid change forced later acceptance of painful readjustments. The American and European automobile industries dominated that world business for decades. Their very existence is now threatened by rising consumer perception that Asian manufacturers offer better products at better prices. The American steel industry suffered similar decline, abetted by the substitution of other materials for traditional uses of steel and the emergence of proficient foreign competitors. Between World Wars One and Two, the French and British armies failed to adapt their force structures and tactics to the potential of air power and armored vehicles, and consequently suffered the great defeats of the early years of World War II. The United States reduced its army to essentially a mobilization base, and also failed to adapt to the utility of aircraft and armor. Similarly, the British and American navies fully accepted the lethality of air delivered weapons against naval warships only after the successes of British naval air attacks against the Italian Navy and Japanese carrier and land-based aircraft successes against them.

I have earlier (in connection with the Japanese attack on Pearl Harbor) referred to the difficulty we humans apparently have in accepting a change or possible change in the existing state of affairs. The "sunk cost fallacy," in which persons continue to sustain a failed investment of capital or time in the hope that it can be recouped, is a similar behavioral phenomenon. Many other examples could be cited. In most cases, there were persons and elements within the organizations whose advocacy of change and adaptation were disregarded in favor of the status quo, often with irreparable damage to their career prospects. "Fallacy" or mere failing, the phenomenon recurs in human affairs, great and small, and deserves our awareness and attention. Critical thinking must include looking toward existing and future conditions and possible need for preparation and adaptation. I have elsewhere referred to the need to assess threats and weaknesses as well as strengths and opportunities. "Constant vigilance," our American forefathers held, "is the price of safety." Of course, "thinking outside the box" toward the future does not necessarily produce brilliant ideas or even good ideas that are suited to a particular organization, circumstance, or time. Any proposed change or innovation will invite and must also withstand critical examination. The important thing is to establish and maintain an atmosphere that welcomes, and critically examines, innovative thinking.

Problems of Persuasive Appeals

The preceding discussion of "thinking inside the box" returns us to the role of emotion in decision making. I earlier asserted that we bring to the decision-making occasion our entire persona, the sum of the parts which make us what we are and determine our predilections, tastes, sympathies, antagonisms, beliefs, hopes and fears. These elements comprise our own intellectual and emotional "box." If we wish to improve as decision-makers, it is well that we understand both ourselves and the nature of influences upon our decision making. Contemporary information collection and storage systems enable supplicants of all kinds to know us, and to direct their efforts to influence our decisions in the light of our known personal emotional and intellectual characteristics. We provide that information directly and indirectly in what we buy, what organizations we join, what policies we support or oppose, what schools we attend or have attended, what occupations and hobbies we pursue, what web sites we visit, where we live, how we live. Computers and the ubiquitous Internet have provided the means to collect, store, and distribute detailed information about us to a level that was unattainable in any previous time. There is nothing inherently wrong with this activity in the moral or ethical sense, and in fact it can be useful to us in bringing matters of interest to us to our attention. But, it may also be useful to be aware that any number of organizations and persons can obtain this knowledge and use it to influence our decisions through appeals to our emotional side. Those persons and organizations are not necessarily our enemies (though some may be), and any one of us may be among those who employ some form of these tactics. But, since we are all vulnerable to appeals to our emotions, it may be well for us to consider the advice of Sun Tzu, author of the oldest known tract on strategy in war: "If you know your enemy and know yourself, you need not fear the result of a hundred battles. If you know yourself but not the enemy, for every battle gained you will also suffer a defeat. If you know neither the enemy nor yourself, you will succumb in every battle." [8] Of course, the act of attempting to motivate us toward a particular decision does not ordinarily constitute an enemy activity, but the parallel exists: if we understand ourselves reasonably well, and understand the appeal that is targeting our emotional self, we may be better able to recognize an emotional appeal and respond to it with the appropriate mix of reason and emotion.

The Decision Making Situation

From the preceding discussion, and from our earlier examination of the problems of filtering useful and reliable information from the flood of misinformation, disinformation, deceit, and various other flotsam and jetsam, it will be seen that the situation of the decision maker is not necessarily a happy one. The decision maker is beset from without by these phenomena, and from within by the human tendency to err. The decision maker, you will remember, is "us." We turn our attention now to the qualities that may enable "us" to do a better job.

Chapter 6

Decision Making and Meetings

ON MEETINGS IN GENERAL

What Is a Meeting?

"What Is a Meeting?" The question at first glance seems unnecessary. We know what meetings are in our place of employment, and we don't particularly care for them. We recognize that they are necessary to both the flow of information and to decision-making, because they bring together persons offering all the necessary different bodies of knowledge and experience. We also recognize that they last too long, feature too much tedium, grandstanding, obstructionism, rude vocal overpowering, and other unproductive annoyances, and accomplish too little for the time and effort expended. We are painfully aware that some participants conduct themselves as players in a game that they must win, rather than a cooperative endeavor.

These are the surface characteristics, the phenomena that meet the visual and auditory senses. If these characteristics are even somewhat accurately descriptive of meetings in your organization and/or consistent with your experience, permit an assurance that the description fits the unsatisfactory meeting. Productive meetings are realizable, necessary, and beneficial to participants. To establish the conditions for the good meeting, one must look beneath the surface characteristics for some underlying realities.

First, let's focus on the meaning, for the purposes of this discussion, of the term "meeting." Webster's New Collegiate dictionary offers: "the act or process of coming together" as "an assembly for a common purpose." Certainly a meeting is a gathering of at least two people, but "coming together" as "an assembly" does not take into account the contemporary ability to hold a "virtual meeting" via telephone, video, or internet conference and the growing use and sophistication of those methods. A further "problem" - if one chooses that description - with Webster's definition is that it allows for any purpose. For example, four friends meet at a local favorite bar for the purpose of drinking beer, or four golfers meet on the first tee, or two lovers meet for romance. All of those may be worthy purposes under the right circumstances, but they are, for our purposes, not meetings. If, on the other hand, we start with the sole criterion as the face-to-face interaction of two or more people, one could reasonably argue that any event that has two or more persons relating to each other conversationally, or otherwise communicating "for a common purpose," is a meeting. The difficulty with that definition is that is would allow a fistfight or a shouting argument to be classified as a meeting. As another example, a football huddle before the subsequent play is rightly regarded as a meeting. A common purpose exists, information is exchanged, a decision is reached, the attendees know their individual and collective purposes and proceed with the effort to accomplish them. But, the subsequent play, although it involves a physical meeting of the two teams, would be more appropriately described as an encounter.

On a larger scene, a formal session of the United States House of Representatives involving a few hundred people is accepted without hesitation as a meeting, but one would hesitate to refer to a sports event involving thousands of spectators as a meeting, although they share the common purpose of viewing the event. Some events that would not ordinarily be classed as meetings can become meetings. For example, two business acquaintances encounter each other by chance, pause to renew acquaintance, find a common problem and common ground, turn on their **Decision Making Mode,** and agree to further discussions regarding both businesses. A family gathers for an evening meal, and the attendant conversation surfaces the need for a decision or decisions with respect to one or more family members.

The preceding should suffice to show that the line one might draw between meetings and human gatherings that are not regarded as meetings is somewhat blurred: some gatherings of people clearly are "meetings," some just as clearly are not, and some must lie in between. For that reason, I have somewhat arbitrarily selected for further examination some events that are, in my view, both useful to our purposes and suitably regarded as "meetings." Our central interest is in meetings, single or repetitive, that are intended to examine a matter and reach a "what to do" decision. A secondary interest lies in meetings that do not necessarily lead to an immediate conclusion, but may expose issues and views and provide experience that will lead in time to decisions.

Good Meetings, Bad Meetings

Good Meetings achieve their purposes, are economical, engage all participants. Participants have been fully informed, well in advance of the meeting, of the purpose and necessary preparation. The agenda has followed the logical problem solving steps:

problems defined and limited, factors identified and evaluated, facts established and assumptions made explicitly, conclusion derived from the process of sharing facts and opinions, and recommendation derived from the conclusion. Time has been budgeted for each topic and the time budget has been met. A time limit of about three hours per session has been set and achieved. The meetings have started on time, ended on time. The chairperson has maintained discipline and kept parties focused but has not dominated the proceeding or outcome. Participants who have sought to dominate the proceedings have been contained, and the chairperson has requested those attendees who have not participated in discussion to provide their views orally, during the meeting. Participants have followed the rules of logical argumentation. The chairperson's summary at the end of each session, and intermittently during sessions, has fairly summarized the discussions, has been pointed and appropriately brief, and has invited assent or dissent. Meeting facilities have been secured against unwanted telephone calls, visitors, and other interruptions. Privacy has been assured (no outside talk about the deliberations). The chairperson has issued calls for papers at appropriate points. Issues have been identified and resolved, or dissents in writing address the unresolved issues. The chairperson has recognized particularly significant contributions, without implying dissatisfaction with other participants. The participants feel satisfaction in their results and management's recognition of their individual and group contributions.

Bad or Unsatisfactory Meetings. The litany of phenomena that can produce unproductive meetings reflects the obverse of the good meeting's characteristics. The litany includes the bad start: unclear directions from above on the meeting's purpose and, either for that reason or others, insufficient advance notification and preparation, and failure in the early sessions to define and limit the problem, clarify the objectives, and obtain management's approval of an agenda that includes a revised objective and deliberative process. Meetings start late, or some participants arrive late and interrupt ongoing discussion. Meetings last too long, lose focus and allow digressions. Participants arrive unprepared, for their own reasons or lack of adequate prior notification of the necessary preparations. The early meetings in a series fail to establish an agenda for a logical problem-solving process. The chairperson wants to use the meeting process to endorse a prior conclusion (one aspect of the poor chairperson). Interruptions, in which one or more participants are called out to address routine problems, are allowed to disrupt or delay deliberations. The chairperson fails to maintain the necessary adherence to logical argumentation. Vocal overpowering, interruptions of speakers, monopolizing the discussion, *ad hominem* arguments, off-topic excursions, fallacious arguments, and a general lack of discipline corrupt the proceedings. One participant or more is deliberately obstructionist, and the chair fails to exercise its options, which include a call for a position paper, to address that matter. The purposes of the meeting, or meetings, has for one or more reasons not been achieved. The experience has left unresolved conflicts and resentments in some participants.

From the preceding discussion, one may reasonably infer that the central (ultimate) reason for bad meeting is lack of training, or lack of a published and disseminated guide emanating from management, on how to conduct oneself as participant or chairperson. Bad meetings produce bad decisions, or no decisions, or waste valuable time and incur excessive cost. Time spent on training all persons who may be participants or chairpersons for decision making meetings therefore appears likely to be a good investment.

Informal Decision-Making Meetings

All organizations are characterized by a structure that is pyramidal in the sense that the number of separate sub-organizations and personnel is greatest at the lowest level or organization and rank. The number of boxes on the organization chart, and the corresponding number of personnel, decrease at each higher level of the organization. It seems likely, therefore, that far more decisions are made at the lower levels, with the matters seen as more important passed from the lower levels to the higher. It is also true that the organizational pyramid is one of age and experience, with the younger and less experienced entering from at the bottom and advancing up the pyramid with experience. The degree of formality of decision-making meetings also moves from the informal and casual at the lowest levels to the more formal, scheduled conference room style at higher levels. At the lower organizations levels, the more common decision-making meetings are those of a manager and one or a few subordinates addressing a particular matter, the small peer group meeting, and less frequently the multi-disciplinary (and possibly multi-session) conference. They represent the meat and potatoes of organizational decision-making: the manager-subordinate meeting addressing the more common decision-making needs, the small peer group meeting addressing matters within a single discipline or activity, and the multi-disciplinary conference method addressing more complex matters. The following discussion therefore concentrates on these forms.

These meetings, which occur innumerable times every business day, are relatively unimportant as single events. Their importance lies first in the fact that they probably address the vast majority of decisions that an organization makes, and, perhaps equally or more important, provide the initial training ground in decision-making in that organization. A positive aspect of these meetings is informality and absence of need for large facilities, administrative help, and formal preparation. They can be set up by phone or network and often resolved in that manner.

The general outlines of a possible way to improve these relatively informal decision-making meetings thus begin to emerge: essentially, retain the informality but give it structure. If one requires a name to describe this concept, call it structured informality. The logical syntax described in earlier chapters provides the basis for the agenda and the structured flow of the meeting. Once more, that syntax is: get the problem understood and rigorously defined → identify and assess the factors that influence the problem and its solution → gather and verify the relevant facts → state the necessary assumptions explicitly → identify and assess the possible solution options → choose one option or a combination of options → incorporate the selected option or options in the proposed "to do" statement. This is not to say that ordinary common sense combined with occupational knowledge never suffices: it merely argues that, if one wishes to improve thousands of decisions, adoption of a structured method and widespread understanding and use of it seems likely to be beneficial. I believe that the structure should include an agenda with time budgeted for each of the steps in the decision-making syntax. This can be done quickly and informally, or in advance of the meeting. It gives direction and flow toward a conclusion, and a sense of the time needed to reach it.

The ordinary, or modal, setting for the manager-subordinate meeting is one in which the manager has a wider range of knowledge, by virtue of experience or special preparation. On the other hand, the manager has wider responsibilities, and for that reason the person who has identified a problem is ordinarily better prepared to provide its details. Accordingly, in a meeting to discuss a problem within the subordinate's field, it is reasonable to expect the subordinate to provide the analysis reiterated in the preceding paragraph. This applies also if the manager has requested the meeting and identified the matters to be addressed. If there has been insufficient time for the subordinate to reason through the matter, the meeting then takes the form of an informal group problem-solving session. To avoid unintentional influence, the manager should not disclose his views on the matter in advance of the decision-making meeting.

Formal Meetings: The Vital Role of the Chairperson

The preceding paragraphs propose some structure for informal decision making meetings. Meetings that address more significant matters and/or involve attendance of higher level personnel, and perhaps require a number of sessions, can benefit from certain additional structural measures. For lack of a better term, I characterize such meetings as "formal."

Formal meetings require a designated chairperson, and often an administrator to manage other necessary activities. The meeting, or first of repetitive meetings, really begins before the first official session, with the chairperson's memorandum to participants and their principals, setting forth the declared purpose, the time and place for the first meeting, and an outline of the plan for continuing after the first meeting if additional meetings are foreseen. A draft agenda, subject to acceptance as the initial act of the conferees, should be part of the advance notification package. The agenda should include a time budget for each topic, and a beginning and end time for the meeting. If appropriate for an initial meeting, the chairperson's memorandum might include a call for position papers.

The agenda for a decision-making discussion, regardless of the level of formality is conceptually always the same logical problem solving syntax. The procedural rules are always those of logical and critical argumentation. Participants must stick to the topic. Assertions (claims) must be defended by their author. Questions of fact or probability that are not resolvable by opinion should be set aside for research and verification. If assumptions must be made, they must be explicit and consistent with what is known. All participants must express their views: the chairperson must demand that they do, and provide opportunity by directly calling upon them to comment. Weak and fallacious arguments must be identified. All comments must be constructive; that is, directed toward advancing the dialogue. Being constructive clearly excludes *ad hominem* attacks, monopolization of conversation/dialogue, resort to rank, rudeness, vocal overpowering, showboating, excessive assertiveness, empty posturing as advocate of truth and justice versus the forces of evil, use of "red herrings" (arguments or topics that lead away from the issue at hand), sophistry in the form of frequent petty objections to various comments, and various other counterproductive behaviors. Participants may be well enjoined to follow the aphorism that their comments should be kind, true, and useful.

Clearly, maintaining the desired conditions depends heavily upon the chairperson. Above all else, the chairperson's responsibility lies in establishing and maintaining the "atmosphere" of rational discussion and civility. The chairperson has the responsibility, and must have the accompanying authority, to enforce the procedural rules. The chairperson's authority should be clearly established in writing by a level of management senior to all participants. If the chairperson has been designated orally by senior management, she should draft the necessary written authority, obtain senior management's signature and support, and circulate the written document to the various entities to be represented in the meeting. The chairperson's responsibility in the meeting or meetings implies, among other things: keeping participants on topic; curtailing excessive speechifying by some; stimulating others by directly asking their opinions; canvassing and summarizing the status of the proceedings periodically during sessions and, in the case of a decision-making conference requiring a number of meetings, at the end of each session; assuring the necessary record-keeping.

The chairperson's end-of-meeting oral summary should outline her views of progress or lack thereof, and what needs to be done in the interim before the next meeting, and in succeeding meetings. It should serve also as a canvassing medium, to allow participants to express their own views. Decision-making or problem solving meetings are ordinarily multi-disciplinary. The conclusions reached will necessarily be a merging of different viewpoints. A consensus may develop and grow as the meetings, or series of meetings, proceeds. The end-of-meeting summary and canvass provides a forum for developing a consensus.

An important associated tool available to the chairperson is the aforementioned "Call for Papers," which may be done orally within the meeting session but also, and always, in writing to the organizations represented by the conferees. The call for papers requires the contributing parties to examine their own prior beliefs and perhaps modify positions previously taken orally. It thus flushes out and formalizes issues. It provides opportunity to address the problem of participants acting under a mandate of their organizational superiors. In parallel, the chairperson should identify and assign a willing participant or other person to draft a "strawman," a draft paper that synthesizes the oral and written comments available. The "strawman" then becomes the locus for further discussion and finalization. If a record is necessary, the chairperson may provide it by means of a memorandum for record or the chairperson's written and circulated summary. Alternatively, verbatim minutes or a summary account provided by a designated recorder provide a more comprehensive and more expensive record. A final duty of the chairperson is to conclude the process: thank participants, recognize important contributions publicly and via correspondence to their parent organizations if appropriate. If the meeting itself is not the decision-maker, the chairperson may have the responsibility to assure decision-maker consideration of the conclusions and recommendations.

Conference type meetings ordinarily require the assignment of an administrator to handle problems of facilities, services, security, privacy, record keeping, correspondence, and similar important activities. Some essential characteristics of the well-conducted conference-type meetings, or series of meetings, are provided below, in the form of a checklist of actions and conditions that should produce better management of the proceedings.

A Conference Check List

Preparatory stage completed: participants notified of the time, place, and purpose

Meeting place secure

Controlled admission

Control of interruptions by telephone or persons

Necessary materials, refreshments available

Agenda with time targets for each topic or problem-solving sequence

Call to order, on time:
introductions (names, organization represented, occupational
& other relevant knowledge).

Chairman's briefing re problem
origins/history, current status, management interest and perception of the problem, approval of agenda

Problem definition
discussion
decision

Factors bearing on the problem
management's concept
stakeholders
    who are they?
    what do they want, expect?
    solution constraints
    money, personnel, policy, internal and external conditions

Solution criteria
    functional design of solution
    important Facts and Assumptions
    solution options
    identify, consider, eliminate, select

Conclusions

Recommendations or decision

The "Side Effects" Utility of Meetings

The significant proportion of meetings that attendees might characterize as "bad" or "unsatisfactory" or "unnecessary" appears to have produced widespread scepticism concerning the value of meetings in general. There are, however, some oblique benefits to meetings or gatherings, even if they might be unsatisfying and unsuccessful in accomplishing their declared purpose, and they merit our notice. Meetings of any kind within an organization get people out of their office or cubicle or home for a time, and can thus instill a sense of belonging that is important to both the individual and the organization. They provide the opportunity for people to interact, to learn something of each other and from each other, and to recognize each other as members of the same team. By acquainting people with each other, and each other's fields of competence, they encourage formation and development of the informal communications system and organization that characterizes successful enterprises. They can break the monotony and isolation of working as a sole individual. Humans are social animals, and meetings provide opportunity for the "socialization" of persons whose ordinary work environment isolates them in cubicles or small offices, or separates them from others in some other way. Meetings provide a means of accomplishing and sustaining their "fit" into the organization as a social group. Through this process, meetings can result in the so-called "cross pollenation of ideas" within an organization, and thus lead to improvements in decision making. So, let's consider several types, which may be useful in the sense of this paragraph, and perhaps also for decision-making, directly or indirectly.

Town Hall Meetings. The title is, of course, borrowed from the traditional practice of some New England communities, in which the entire citizenry is invited to participate and make decisions, by majority vote, with respect to matters of community concern. The version we are here addressing is a meeting of an entire organization's personnel, or a large homogenous group (e. g., all of a brokerage house's securities analysts, all of a manufacturer's service engineers), sometimes requiring separate sessions to accommodate the large number of people involved. For a variety of reasons, "town meetings" are ordinarily held only for some special and out-of-the-ordinary purpose. The purposes might include: to announce contemplated or actual major changes or developments and obtain "grass-roots's" views and support, to quell rumors, to provide information regarding the organization's status and prospects, to invite comments regarding opportunities to correct or improve any aspect of employment, or simply to expose the organization's senior leadership, and personnel who do not ordinarily have direct contact with it, to each other. The beneficial side of such meetings is that all participants receive and store information and hear views that would ordinarily reach them slowly and incompletely, if at all, and with some distortion. They may also serve to convince lower echelons that the leadership's decisions are rationally based, that the top echelons are mindful of the opinions and interests of lower echelons, and that the issues that emerge will receive management attention. They may also convince the leadership that their decisions have satisfactory support, and thus contribute to managerial vigor. An unintended consequence may be that the occasion provides opportunity for direct and impassioned venting of complaints by members of the audience, deviations from the meeting's planned topics, and failure to accomplish the aims of the meeting, with subsequent lessening of confidence in the leadership and/or its decisions. If that phenomenon does arise, the leadership will have learned something important for its future decision making. The high cost of such large meetings of an organization's personnel is always an adverse factor.

The Post-Operation Critique, or *Debriefing.* This relative of the Town Hall meeting brings together all or most of the key participants in a particular operation or endeavor - for example, a military mission or a large construction project, a marketing campaign, or an athletic contest - to express their views as to how well or badly they or others performed, and how they and the entire organization might improve performance in the future. Its usefulness is dependent upon encouraging all participants, down to the lowest level, to offer criticisms of the planning and execution of the operation at all levels. Conducted under the rules of rational argumentation, the *post-operation critique* is a useful, often necessary, means of identifying opportunities to improve performance. A form of this meeting type is the weekly or daily review meeting.

The Huddle. Unless you have spent until yesterday on another and distant planet, you will have witnessed the use of the huddle in athletic events, particularly football, any number of times. *The huddle* in athletics has its less-well-recognized counterparts in other forms of human endeavor: the morning meeting in the senior official's office, the shift-change meeting in continuous operations, the late Friday meeting summing-up the week's performance. *The Huddle* in football and other sports has positive effects apart from its communication of what to do next. It provides, perhaps more than any other form of meeting, for each participant a sense of belonging, of being part of a team, of relying on other team members and in turn deserving and earning their confidence and reliance. The frequent repetition reinforces that sense of united effort, and enhances each member's confidence in others and in his own performance. *The Huddle* form is, then, not only a vital means of communication: it is also a team builder. Replicating it in some form suitably adapted to the organization can provide similar benefits.

The Morning Meeting in the senior official's office is a close relative of *The Huddle*. Sometimes devised as *The Stand-up Meeting* (because all participants except the senior official stand, somewhat in a semicircle around the senior official's desk), it brings together a senior manager and those directly reporting to him for a sharing of important news of the day, or pertinent instructions or decisions, or anything of interest to other group members. It can also serve as a motivating session, setting production or sales goals or other objectives for the day. Apart from its advantages in cross-communicating, it affords opportunity for the senior manager to see subordinates at the beginning of each work day, and subordinates to see their manager and each other and become accustomed and comfortable with daily contact. It provides a daily reminder of who the team members are, what the organization's current problems and objectives are, and what is to be done to address them in the short term. It is, or can be, thus an important team-building tool. By bringing the participants briefly into close physical proximity, it provides the team-building and decision making features of its close relative, *The Huddle*. The *Stand-Up* format emphasizes the purpose of keeping the meeting as brief as possible.

The Morning Briefing. A more formal version of the morning meeting, the morning or pre-shift briefing provides a prepared presentation, or "briefing," to illuminate any and all matters that require the attention or knowledge of the attendees. The briefing may provide a situation assessment or situation update on any topics of interest. The briefing can provide information supporting, or requiring, a decision, and in that sense the briefing session becomes a decision-making session. Like the other morning meetings, it can serve as a unifying and team-building instrument. Attendees can include not only the principals involved in the necessary decision-making, but also selected advisers and junior personnel whose development may be enhanced by attendance and observation, but not necessarily participation. In that usage, it can provide a beneficial means for more junior personnel to become acquainted with both the information and the decision-making process. The potential benefits depend, of course, on the quality of the information presented and the decision-making process.

Brainstorming Meetings. In the second half of the Twentieth Century, "brainstorming" became a hit method of eliciting ideas. The concept: to assemble a number of people, often representing different fields of knowledge, in a conference room, outline a particular problem or topic, and ask that the participants suspend their critical faculties in favor of their creative side and offer any ideas that spring to their minds. Any and all ideas are recorded, with critical appraisal to follow in a separate session or sessions, perhaps with different participants. Obviously, the method offers opportunity to elicit useful ideas. The interplay of minds may stimulate spontaneity and "thinking outside the box" that daily routine does not encourage. Its negative aspects include the following:

a) some participants are reluctant to offer ideas that they have been developing but they perceive as unready for publication;

b) the source of good ideas may be obscured by the group process, with the result that participants, particularly those who have been working for some time on the matter and have developed some well-considered approaches, may feel that the process precludes any tangible or intangible reward for their contribution, and/or that others may claim credit for their ideas;

c) ideas that have potential but are not accepted for action may be discarded and thus discredited, and their further development terminated;

d) the format invites ill-considered ideas: persons who offer ideas that are far outside "the Box" may become objects of ridicule after the meeting;

e) above all else, the format assumes that the problem is identified and understood, and thus may skip the vital first step in problem solving as well as the succeeding steps in an orderly decision making process. Brainstorming is essentially an elicitation of solution options, without having assured understanding of the problem to be addressed.

Some of these disadvantages may be overcome by procedural methods, but a "working group" or "study group" using the structured decision-making methodology seems significantly superior, because it incorporates the creative search for options into a larger logical syntax. Options may then be proposed in a brainstorming session, or in response to the chairman's call for papers, providing some assurance to their originators that their contributions will be appropriately recognized.

A Conclusion and Recommendation

Good meetings derive from the behavior of the chairperson and participants, as do unsatisfactory meetings. Behavior can be improved, and performance and productivity improved accordingly, by training prospective participants and chairpersons. The material on good meetings in this chapter, if adopted as a standard for behavior, can lead to significant improvement in group decision-making. If a broader program seems in order, a formal training program incorporating the same measures and a broader range of material can be adopted by large organizations.

Chapter 7

The Decision Maker Concept

KNOW THE ENEMY, KNOW THYSELF

The "Good" Decision-Maker Mode

In our earlier dipping into the stream of human thought, we encountered the philosophical argument that an important element of our knowledge is self-knowledge. Further, we found a seeming consensus that self-knowledge must be frequently refreshed by self-examination, which can lead to better understanding of our strengths, our limitations, our opportunities for development, and those personal characteristics that threaten our development and perhaps our prospects in life. That leads to the matter of defining, however roughly, the personal qualities that should characterize the "good" decision-making mode. What qualities are useful, what should be suppressed or muted?

To reiterate earlier observations: that fictitious figure who is stand-in for all of us, the human decision maker, should reach decisions through a process. For many of us, the process is random and haphazard. If you've read this far and I've done my job, you should be convinced that the process ought to be structured and rational, and you are familiar with such a process and the need to incorporate it in one's decision-making mode. The decision-making occasion should prompt one to bring to bear that process, plus other critical faculties and the relevant knowledge stored in one's memory. I have stressed the strong influence of what we carry around in our mental baggage. One cannot totally clear one's mind of preconceptions and firm beliefs, making one's mind a "tabula rasa" (clean slate) for the facts and assumptions regarding each new decision. On the other hand, applying only one's preconceptions may simply result in an habitual use of casuistry (applying a preconceived principle or doctrine) in place of judgment on the facts and merit of the proposed decision. Improving one's decision-making proficiency, then, requires time and sustained effort and appropriate measures of humility. It demands a continuing process of "creative destruction," critically examining what we hold in our mental storage, adding new data and beliefs that will enhance our ability to make "good" decisions. But, if we wish to make "good" decisions, we must have a clear picture of what we mean by that term, beyond our understanding of "good" as distinct from "bad."

"Good" Decisions

Almost every field of thought that has engaged the human mind has addressed decision-making in some manner. Philosophy, psychology, politics, law, religion, operations research, mathematics, management and other fields have attempted in some fashion to define decisions that are "good." In earlier chapters, I suggested a standard: the action or inaction decided upon had to be feasible, practicable, moral, ethical, legal and - taken in its entirety -

reasonable. I also noted that all decisions involve both desired and undesired consequences, and one measure of the "good" decision is that the desired consequences must outweigh the undesired, according to some criteria. It is also true that the desired consequences may accrue to one interest group, the undesired may be borne by another, raising the question of "good" in the minds of the disadvantaged group. I also noted that he frequent occurrence of unforeseen consequences establishes the need for "what could go wrong?" analysis.

The operations research concept of the "payoff function" and the "measure of effectiveness" represent that discipline's manner of defining the "good" in decision-making as accomplishing a particular purpose. In everyday usage, and in pragmatism, the standard is similar: a "good" decision is one that achieves a desired purpose. For some situations and decisions, a wider view may be a necessary quality of the decision making mode. A decision may affect many different individuals and organizations, as well as the general public, and the "good" decision must accord with their concept of the good or, at the very least, not fail to take their views into account. The early Greek philosophers, from whom the modern world has drawn much of its thought, did recognize that need. They inquired into both particular "good ends" - those concerned with a practical matter, as the "payoff function" - and the "universal good" for mankind. The concept was, very broadly, that decision-making with respect to any particular matter had to accord with some standard for the "universal good." Examples of private decisions with broad public interest abound in contemporary life: for example, the placement of a large store or shopping area, the wages paid by a private employer to its employees, the merging of two private enterprises, the compensation of senior corporate executives. Aristotle began his *Nichomachean Ethics* with the keynote observation "that every activity, artistic or scientific, in fact every deliberate action or pursuit, has for its object the attainment of some good." The "good" is that "at which all things aim," but the "ends" (the things aimed at) differ for particular activities: "the end of medical science is health;" of military science, victory; of economic science, wealth. Aristotle then pursues the broad question of whether there is a universal "good," or end, for human activity, and suggests that it must be happiness (although the Greek word Aristotle used is said to be better translated as "well-being").[1] Western philosophy, psychology, political science, and other disciplines have continued the quest for both the universal "good" and for particular "good" ends and means that accord with their concept of a universal "good." Our present-day concept of business and professional ethics reflects a similar pursuit.

Other traditions of thought have addressed the matter: Confucius, still enormously influential in parts of Asia, was concerned in the sixth and fifth centuries before the Christian era with how one may "cultivate virtue," do what is "right," and "conquer" oneself.[2] Confucius is said to have freed himself of four things: "opinionatedness, dogmatism, obstinacy, and ego." He refers to humility in his comment that "A man of humanity, wishing to establish himself, also establishes others, and wishing to enlarge himself, also enlarges others." Siddhartha Gautama (The Buddha), born in India several centuries before the Christian era, held that everything is constantly changing. Humans therefore have "no self" (no permanent set of personal qualities or attributes) because the human personality is, like everything else, in a process of constant change. If change is inevitable and constant, it followed that people have innumerable possibilities. They should therefore take charge of the process within themselves and try to change in positive ways. Buddha's early preaching (some time between 500 B.C. and 350 B.C.)

advocated the "Eightfold Path": right views, right intention, right speech, right action, right livelihood, right effort, right awareness, and right concentration.

These and other inquiries, extending over many cultures, geographic regions, and centuries, offer convincing evidence that humans far removed from each other by distance, culture, and time have sought a moral and rational frame of reference for particular decision-making. Our era of rapid and wide flow of information has intensified this search: decisions that might in the past have been viewed as private are now perceived, particularly in democratic societies, as important business of the public. A private organization's "good" decision is, increasingly, one that recognizes the public's demand that institutional decisions reflect a "good" society. The "good" decision-maker must be, perforce, a person or institution whose decision-making mode includes awareness and understanding of that consideration.

Let us seek further for attributes of the good individual human decision-maker.

The Twentieth Century German philosopher Josef Pieper has illuminated some aspects of that search that may be useful.[3] For Pieper, as for a host of other philosophers over many centuries, these qualities are "the Virtues," by which he meant positive attributes of the human character. The "cardinal virtues" are those that largely define a person's character by their presence, or absence, or lapses in their observation. They are: Prudence, Justice, Fortitude, and Temperance, qualities that have engaged philosophers and thinkers through much of mankind's history. Pieper perceived the four as essentially linked, as necessarily present and active in the same person. Pieper was addressing the virtues in an abstract way, using the method of critical philosophy to explore what the cardinal virtues are and of what qualities they are composed. Applying his categories to the decision-making function, his decision-maker would be prudent (duly cautious and thorough rather than hasty or reckless or overly bold). Prudence must extend to all the other virtues. Justice, Fortitude, and Temperance cannot exist, he held, in the absence of Prudence. Pieper's decision-maker would be just (giving every person his/her due, which might be comprised of reward, punishment, or other form of recognition). His decision maker would have Fortitude, the courage to decide for the right and just and to adhere to the decision in the face of criticism and opposition. Endurance and Attack are components of fortitude: the capacity and determination to endure dangers and go forward to attack them. Pieper's decision-maker would be temperate, not inclined to excesses of emotion or of satisfaction of the concupiscent appetites.

Prudence, Pieper states, "informs" the other virtues: it is the "measure" of justice, of fortitude, of temperance. Prudence determines, in concrete circumstances, how those virtues apply. He perceives prudence as being comprised of three elements that he identifies by their Latin terms: memoria, solertia, docilitas. "Memoria" is a habit of "true-to-being" memory, of accepting and retaining facts as they are, not twisting or gradually altering them in one's mind so as to produce a flawed conception of reality.[4] "Solertia" is the ability to "decide for the good," avoiding injustice, cowardice, and intemperance. This requires, in turn, physical and psychological health. The concept is that of the judicious and just person, courageous enough to make and adhere to an unpopular decision if it is deemed to be the right one, not governed by the desire for personal gain or gratification, not suffering physical illness or mental turmoil or serious aberrations.

"Docilitas" is an important element of prudence: it is the sustained quality of open-mindedness, readiness to seek advice and counsel, receptivity to new facts and ideas, and search for real understanding. The quality necessarily includes humility, an absence of hubris. A closed mind, an attitude of "knowing it all," are forms of resistance to reality. Contemporary dictionaries define prudence as "the ability to govern and discipline oneself by the use of reason" and as "marked by circumspection." Pieper addresses a fourth quality: "providentia." Providentia is perceived as attention to what may develop or occur, "what is still to be realized": foresight, calculation of effects and consequences of a particular action. ("Providentia" necessarily incorporates our earlier comment regarding the necessity for explicit assumptions and "what could go wrong" analysis.)

The enemy of prudence is of course its opposite, imprudence, which for Pieper assumes many forms: thoughtlessness, indecisiveness, negligence, blindness to concrete realities, cunning, intrigue, "tactics," in the end: covetousness. For Pieper, covetousness is a very broad category, incorporating "immoderate striving" for possessions, status, importance, wealth, various other forms of gratification, confirmation and security.

There are, of course, many virtues lesser than the cardinal ones. A few are worth our notice here. Magnanimity refers to greatness of mind, the inclination to live an honorable life. Magnificence largely applies to persons of wealth or affluence who direct their wealth to worthy purposes. Perseverance inclines one to persist in achieving a difficult "good." Each of the virtues has, of course, its opposite.

As a final comment, Pieper recognized the role of "fortuna," by which he meant the unplanned and unanticipated in human lives. By implication, his good decision maker would be aware of the role of uncertainty and "chance" or "luck" or "probability" in deciding for the good. He would recognize the probability and probable consequences of being right, and the probability and probable consequences of being wrong, and factor those probabilities into his decision. Certainty cannot be attained, but the prudent person avoids false expectations and is aware of the potential for undesired and unanticipated consequences. This thought implies, in contemporary terms, consideration of *a priori* probabilities and risk/gain analysis.

The reader will have perceived that the cardinal virtues are qualities that we would describe in ordinary terms as those of the "good man" or "good woman," thoughtful and conscientious persons comfortable with themselves while continuing to strive for personal development. Pieper has much more to offer on these matters from a philosophical viewpoint than one can usefully condense here, and the reader can hardly fail to benefit from reading the work cited, and more particularly his four original works on the "virtues."

The Good Decision-Maker: A First Approximation

The philosophers have given us at least the beginnings of a paradigm for the good decision-maker. Let us here attempt a first approximation. We can easily agree that the good decision-maker is prudent, just, courageous, and self-disciplined. But, in the context we are here addressing, what sort of person do these attributes imply? Prudence in this context means being neither excessively bold nor excessively cautious, neither excessively quick to decide nor excessively given to procrastinate, habituated to a structured decision making process. That person is receptive to advice and counsel and seeks it, particularly on matters that lie outside his sphere of knowledge. On the other hand, the prudent person perceives the need for critical thinking and verification as applying to received advice and counsel as well as to alleged facts and necessary assumptions. The good decision-maker inspires confidence, in those affected by his decisions, that their views and concerns will be sought out and considered; that he will neither lead them into reckless ventures nor take excessive counsel of the dangers which accompany any human action; that he will make and adhere to unpopular decisions if the proposed option meets the tests described earlier (feasible, practicable, legal, moral, ethical, reasonable); that he will not be deflected or governed by excesses in his personal life. That description necessarily implies a serious person, responsible, given neither to frivolity nor excessive self-importance, and constantly seeking improvement. It does not, however, require that the good decision-maker have no other aspects to his persona, or that he or she must always display a serious demeanor, sometimes referred to as "looking as wise as a tree-full of owls." The good decision-maker can also be the good companion, can be fun loving when the time is right for it, can have all the human passions and partake of all life's delights without falling victim to excesses. The **decision-making mode** is a part of the good decision-maker's persona, not the whole, and the good decision-maker will be aware of the occasion to switch to that mode. We are all many things, and one can have many modes other than the decision-making mode.

Shakespeare's Good Decision Maker

Let us turn now to literature for some illumination of the question of individual character as related to decision-making. Here Shakespeare's Hamlet is speaking of Horatio, who is approaching but is beyond the sound of Hamlet's voice. Hamlet describes Horatio: "as just a man" as he had encountered in his life; as one who, suffering all, had suffered nothing; one who had taken "fortune's buffets and rewards" with equal thanks; "whose blood and judgment are so well commingled" that "fortune's finger" could do what it would, without effect. Hamlet then, speaking directly to the arriving Horatio, concludes his greeting:

Give me that man
That is not passion's slave, and I will wear
him
In my heart's core, ay, in my heart of heart,
As I do thee . . .[5]

Shakespeare's Horatio and Pieper's "prudent" man bear close resemblance. In them "Blood and judgment" - emotions, passions, matters of the heart, joined with the mental qualities of prudence, justice, temperance, and fortitude - are blended in a self-possessed (not self-satisfied) person, at peace within, ready to confront what may come.

In the same play, the character Polonious advises his son, Laertes, upon decisions the latter must make in his prospective residence in Paris. This has been scoffed at by some modern critics as ill-equipping Laertes for the presumed sophistication and intrigue of Paris during that period, but I believe it sheds some useful light on our topic, as a brief prescription for prudent behavior in a particular practical application. Here are some excerpts:

"Give thy thoughts no tongue, nor any unproportion'd thought his act." In contemporary language, exercise some restraint: don't speak or act without considering the appropriateness of the contemplated statement or act.

Polonius continues:

"Those friends thou hast, and their affection tried,
Grapple them to thy soul with hoops of steel;
But do not dull thy palm with entertainment
Of each new-hatch'd, unfledged comrade. Beware

of entrance to a quarrel, but being in,
Bear't that the opposed may beware of thee.
Give every man thy ear, but few thy voice:
Take each man's censure, but reserve thy
    judgment.
Costly thy habit as thy purse can buy,
But not express'd in fancy; rich, not gaudy,
For the apparel oft proclaims the man . . .
Neither a borrower nor a lender be;
For loan oft loses both itself and friend,
And borrowing dulls the edge of husbandry.
This above all: to thine own self be true,
And it shall follow, as the night the day,
Thou cans't not then be false to any man.[6]

The Good Decision Maker: Continuing the Search in Onself

"To thine own self be true." Shakespeare, in here describing a set of attributes to guide Laertes' decisions, has applied several concepts. By implying that Laertes can adopt a pattern of behavior that will better equip him to his new environment, Shakespeare recognizes that the "self" is impermanent; it is both malleable and in frequent need of improvement and adaptation to changed circumstances. Second, the "self" can and should take control of the process of improvement and adaptation. Shakespeare's concepts parallel the Buddhist view of the "self" as impermanent, and suggest the benefits to be gained by recurrent self-examination, visualization of the future self one wishes to become, and identification of the measures necessary to effect that transition. The self incorporates, for both individuals and organizations, that set of beliefs and convictions that led Herbert Simon to use the term "bounded" in connection with rationality.

Having accepted the view that persons and organizations can improve by self-examination, the concern then arises: how can the creative destruction and renewal of the self be managed? Must one find a mountain, climb to the top, and ponder the vastness and complexities of the universe in comparison to one's insignificance? Spend a year in solitary thought? Read the many books and blogs concerning self-improvement, watch the television programs and DVD's, listen to the radio programs and lectures? Or, some or none of the above?

We are here entering a topic of considerable significance and concern that has a long history in human affairs: the "examined life." A familiar example in Western culture is Socrates' comment: "The unexamined life is not worth living."[7] Socrates has something to say to us across the millennia and centuries: he provided us a methodology. The objective of the so-called Socratic method was, and is, to help individuals gain self-knowledge through interrogation. Socrates' method was essentially insistent critical interrogation of others, to force them to examine what they believe and logically justify their beliefs. Self-examination requires that we direct the interrogation to ourselves.

The self-examination method is essentially that of the "Situation Audit," factor analysis process earlier described. A good problem statement may be as "To develop an understanding of where I am in life, how I got where I am, whither am I tending, what I need to do to improve, and how to do it?" We humans are, in a meaningful sense, composed of parts: the physical, intellectual, and moral among them. We have roles in life: husband/wife, father/mother, son/daughter, brother/sister, manager, employee, citizen, friend, and so forth. For purposes of self-analysis and personal improvement, our physical, intellectual, and moral selves and the important roles we play in life may be addressed as "factors." Moreover, each of those roles has a number of attributes. A parent may be a provider, a teacher, a disciplinarian, a counselor, a motivator, a companion, inevitably a role model, and a variety of other things. One examines and evaluates one's performance in each of the significant roles one plays. By evaluating performance in <u>all</u> the major roles, one is able to recognize good or acceptable performance in one role at the expense of neglecting another. For example, one may deserve accolades for superior job performance, gained by overtime, weekend work, taking work home, and so forth, at the expense of having neglected one's role as spouse, parent, lover, companion, friend, adviser, or citizen. The situation audit should disclose the imbalances. So, the factors examined should include all the important roles and the balance or lack of balance between them. There also may be imbalances within roles: for example, as a parent.

Because it is more effective to look forward with reasonable expectations rather than backward to what one should have done but failed to perceive, greater and more lasting benefits should be expected from conducting the situation audit and formulating the life plan early in one's independent life and career, and repeating the process periodically. (I employ the term "life plan" to the scope of the plan, addressing all the roles one plays in life, rather than lifetime duration.) Circumstances and inclination permitting, it may be useful to take a few days and remove oneself some distance away from present surroundings and work, on the premise that this change will facilitate viewing oneself and one's situation in life as a detached observer. If there is a significant other who would be affected by any decisions to change, a joint effort to produce a situation audit and life plan for both may be advisable. A detached view may also be facilitated by viewing oneself from the standpoint of a third person addressing the situation of Jane Doe and/or John Doe. The participants might spend a long weekend away from their usual surroundings, and devote a part of it to produce a situation audit and life plan for each participant and fit them together. The analysis should include assessing the SWOT factors, in terms of the participants' existing and prospective situations. The process should lead to a better understanding of where one is strong, where one is weak, where the opportunities lie, what threats exist and how serious and how imminent they are. What are the options, and which ones should be selected? In terms of career, some useful questions to address include the following. Am I in the right career, right job, right place? Am I well prepared to advance within my career field? In what activities or pursuits am I competitive, or superior, or noncompetitive? Do I need to become competitive, or superior? How? What are my principal strengths, and how can they be better applied? What do I need to stop doing, what do I need to start doing? Apart from, and within, my career, am I a decent person? Where am I with respect to possessing and manifesting qualities that humans have learned to respect, such as character, integrity, truthfulness, adherence to careful statement, self-confidence without hubris, job knowledge, next-job knowledge? What are my short-term and long-term objectives, and what measure must I adopt, what measures must I abjure, to attain them?

Having made those judgments, one is then better positioned to develop a plan to be followed for some time, and if there is a significant other, to develop a plan for each that accommodates the other's plan. If minor children or other dependents would be affected, their views and concerns are considerations. One's plan may be formal or informal, written or mentally absorbed, intended for the foreseeable future or indefinite. The objective is to identify any necessary changes or shifts in emphasis. The high probability of change in external conditions suggests the necessity for periodic reviews and adjustments.

In confronting oneself, one is confronted with the question of what to do with one's life, and that forces one to decide on one's definition of the good life. The philosophers and theologians have engaged these questions as long as man has recorded thoughts, without discovering universal answers. Our American *Declaration of Independence* merely allows each of us "the pursuit of happiness," as each of us chooses to define happiness. Aristotle's comment that the manner of a man's life reflects his view of happiness illustrates a similar lack of a universal definition. It does not reflect the constraints one faces in deciding on one's version of the good life: one can only select from the options that are open.

A "mini" situation audit, conducted Friday evening or on the weekend, can be a useful addition to the more comprehensive audit outlined above. The questions one might ask include: "How did I do this past week, how can I improve? What did I learn that should become part of my store of knowledge? What did I learn about my occupation, my colleagues, my family and friends, myself?"

Allow a few caveats. Critical self-examination, honestly conducted, should ordinarily expose aspects of oneself that are less than admirable. We are, after all, imperfect, and our self-examination merely provides some specifics. Some regret and chagrin may result from our meeting with ourselves, and those emotions can usefully inspire our efforts to improve. Excessive dwelling on them may reopen old wounds, to the detriment of our purpose. This is a matter in which the saying "When life knocks you down, pick yourself up, dust yourself off, and go on" applies for most of us. We wanted to find out where we needed improvement, and we got the desired result. Self-examination does not suggest a need to remake one's entire personality. It is simply a repetitive effort to examine one's views, biases, prejudices, beliefs, emotional attachments , in a detached way, to discard those which are mistaken or no longer applicable, and to adopt those that pass the test of critical examination. Regardless of the initial motivation, self-examination is an occasion for critical philosophy, for on the one hand being receptive to new information to store in memory, and on the other hand subjecting the new information to critical examination.

If, on the other hand, critical self-examination exposes nothing about oneself but wholly admirable traits and performance, one has possibly discovered a case of hubris. As with a medical diagnosis, a second opinion, or several opinions, might be illuminating. The poet Robert Burns' comment, in his 1786 poem *To a Louse*, addresses the problem:

> Oh wad some power the giftie gie us
> To see oursels as others see us!
> It wad frae monie a blunder free us,
> An' foolish notion.

A recheck, starting with one's self-image, accompanied by input from others, may be appropriate.

The Good Decision Maker: A Concluding Approximation

We have moved forward in our search for a set of qualities that characterize the good decision maker. We cannot, of course, identify and describe all the qualities that might characterize such a person, but we can reach some conclusions regarding the essentials.

The good decision maker has performed a self-assessment, perhaps through a process similar to that outlined in the preceding section. She has established goals and plans for her own life and career, and determined firmly what she will do, and will not do, to attain those goals. She has established her character and standard of performance in each of her roles in life. Her constant concern is to decide and act responsibly, to live an honorable life. Her persona - her "social facade," what she appears to be to others - accords with what she is, her so-called inner self. She has taken charge of her life, and responsibility for it.

The good decision-maker has a **Decision-Making Mode** and the ability to recognize an important decision-making occasion and switch to that mode. She is proactive in seeking out matters that may benefit by examination and decision. She is self-possessed, doesn't become slave to any of the emotions or to fixed beliefs. The good decision-maker is aware of her own situation and limitations: her strengths, weaknesses, opportunities, threats; where she is in life and career, and whither she is tending. She engages in continuous renewal of her knowledge and belief base, to adjust to existing and anticipated changes in the "state of nature" and to avoid hubris and the other "deadly sins." She maintains a balance of self-confidence and humility and looks to the strengths in others to provide knowledge she lacks. She is a critical thinker, recognizing emotional and fallacious arguments, unverified "facts," and implicit assumptions. She understands and employs the decision making syntax: get the problem properly understood and stated, break it into factors, develop the necessary facts and explicit assumptions regarding the factors, identify the options and select one or a combination that best promises to achieve the desired results and, upon critical review, passes the "what could go wrong" and the "feasible, practicable, legal, moral, ethical, and reasonable" tests.

In a position of leadership, she recognizes the importance of that decision making structure and the positive influence of wide recognition that her organization has a structured decision-making process: rational, visible, published and taught and practiced within the organization. She knows how and under what circumstances to conduct a situation audit, how to use the knowledge gained from it to develop a realistic plan that includes the objectives to be attained, the means to be used to attain them, and the time schedule for various key achievements. She understands that a plan is a "To Do" list: the first step in the management cycle of planning, organizing, staffing, directing, monitoring, readjusting. She encourages the use of informal logic and the rules of argumentation throughout her organization. She is aware of the potential benefits of the Socratic method, employed without giving offense by simply questioning the basis of assertions of fact or opinion. She seeks and respects good counsel, is willing to change her views and her perception of the contemporary "state of nature." She listens well, and engages the speaker in dialogue according to the rules of constructive informal logic. In seeking and accepting counsel, she does not become dependent upon one or a few counselors and recognizes the dangers of single-valued arguments and her own suggestibility.

She has a repertoire of decision tradecraft and draws upon it as appropriate. She is aware of the "satisficer" tendency, and therefore identifies and evaluates all options. She recognizes the forms of special pleading and errors of method such as casuistry and sophistry. On those occasions when her principal role is that of final decision-maker, she is careful not to show predisposition toward any particular option. She understands the uses of probability and the potential and dangers of its Bayesian version. She is aware of transactional options (act for act, act for promise, promise for promise, promise for act), and understands the dangers of performing acts in return for promises. She understands the economics of decision-making (time, money, effort, opportunity cost, versus value of outcome), knows that elaborate techniques (modeling, gaming, formal debate, mathematical analysis, outside experts) are expensive and time-consuming, and therefore reserves their use for decisions of great importance and complexity. She avoids both unnecessary haste and unnecessary delay. She makes her decision when, or before, the time available for making it has been exhausted, or when all the necessary facts and assumptions have been carefully and critically examined, all factors taken into account, all options examined and re-examined, and further effort promises negligible gain. She knows enough, understands enough, and knows she knows and understands enough. She must now decide, and she does so with determination to carry out the decision.

That observation leads to a final point. In keeping with earlier comments that all managers do not do the same things, and that each of us is manager of our self and our life, I have provided a broad selection of decision making tradecraft and concepts, from which one may select an applicable set. I have ventured some safe distance into a number of disciplines, enough to suggest how much more remains to be learned in a life and career. We are thus approaching a departure point. If you, valued reader, have found in this brief volume some knowledge that you wish to add to your store, if you are confident that you know enough and understand enough, you must now decide what to retain, structure, and employ. We have identified the major questions that confront us throughout our journey. Where am I in life and work? Whither am I tending? Where do I want to be? How and when do I plan to get there? The questions always confront us, but in the unexamined life we do not confront them: we drift with the tides of life, going where they take us. In the examined life, we confront those questions, taking as much control as circumstances permit, recognizing the ring of truth in both Shakespeare's comment that we can only "rough hew' our ends and Sartre's that we can have no other aim than that we set for ourselves, no other destiny than that we forge for ourselves. In the next brief and final chapter, I offer a structure, in an outline form of the entire management cycle, for addressing these questions. I have followed Einstein's injunction, quoted in the preface to this book, to make it as simple as possible, but not more so. It makes no attempt to identify any final or even interim objectives for one's career or life. It merely opens a path the reader may take toward aims one must define for oneself.

Chapter 8

Managing Life and Work: Encapsulated

A MANAGEMENT PLAN

This book has asserted that management and decision making are inseparable: when we speak or write of the one, we imply also the other. It has also asserted that we are all managers, in the sense of managing ourselves and our lives. The essence of management has elsewhere been tersely but well described as "getting the right things done right." That implies deciding what the right things to do are, and how and when to do them right. The steps necessary to identify the right things to do, and to get them done right, are easily identified and have been verified by long experience. I outline them below, in the form of a structured approach for making those decisions:

If:

upon assuming a first or new management assignment or new situation in your life, you conduct a comprehensive and competent situation audit, and update it as necessary;

and,

from the knowledge thus gained, you define and limit the problems to be addressed;

and,

you develop a realistic plan that includes the objectives to be attained, the means to be used to attain them, and the time schedule for various key achievements;

and,

you then organize your own and/or your organization's efforts on the basis of the objectives to be attained and the means available or procurable to attain them;

and,

(if management is your job) you hire or assign or contract for people with the necessary skills and motivation to accomplish the required tasks;

and,

you provide clear direction to the people assigned;

and,

you establish and maintain a monitoring system that provides a continuous measure of progress toward the objectives;

and,

you make the necessary readjustments and assignments that your measurement of progress indicates;

and,

you select, fit to your circumstances, and apply a suitable set of the measures outlined in this book;

and,

you also exercise common sense and common decency in performing these actions;

THEN,

you have a good chance of doing a respectable job of all the steps outlined above, and that amounts to doing a good job of managing;

And if,

you use the same sequence, suitably adjusted, to managing your own development and responsibilities;

THEN,

if your job is management, you have a good chance of improving your capacity to perform managerial duties at progressively higher levels of responsibility;

and,

you may find greater satisfaction in your life's work;

and,

whatever your job, you will have examined your life, and you may do a better job of living it.

Endnotes

CHAPTER 1

1. Aristotle, *The Nicomachean Ethics*, in J. A. K. Thomson (trans.), *The Ethics of Aristotle* (Baltimore: Penguin Books, 1958), p. 30.

2. See, for example, Irving L. Janis and Leon Mann, *Decision-Making: A Psychological Analysis of Conflict, Choice, and Commitment* (New York: The Free Press, 1979), esp. 15, 26, 132; Ben Heirs and Gordon Pehrson, *The Mind of the Organization*. Rev. ed. (New York Harper and Row Publishers, 1982), esp. p. xxii; Norman S. Sutherland, *Irrationality: Why we don't think straight* (New Brunswick, N. J.: Rutgers University Press, 1994).

3. Herbert Simon and Associates, *Decision Making and Problem Solving*. Reprint with permission from *Research Briefings 1986: Report of the Research Briefing Panel on Decision Making and Problem Solving*. Washington, D. C.: National Academy Press, 1986.

CHAPTER 2

1. "The Power of Design," *BusinessWeek*, May 17, 2004, p. 86.

2. Calpine Corporation 10 K/A filing with SEC, September 22, 2004, pp. 4–5.

3. "Marketplace by Bloomberg," *Bloomberg News,* December 22, 2005.

CHAPTER 3

1. See Thomas Sowell, *Knowledge and Decisions* (New York, N.Y.: Basic Books, 1996, pp. 11–14 and *passim.*

2. A publication with enduring relevance, is Patrick H. Irwin, *Business Planning: Key to Profit Growth* (Toronto, Winnipeg, Vancouver: Society of Industrial Accountants of Canada and the Myerson Press, 1970.

CHAPTER 4

1. Rene_ Descartes, "Discourse On Method," (trans. Laurence J. Lafleur. _____, Liberal Arts Press, Inc., 1956), p. 12.

2. Ibid..

3. David Klein and Marymae Klein, *How Do You Know It's True?* (New York: Charles Scribner's Sons, 1984), p. 59.

4. Washington Post Foreign Service, June 13, 2007, p. A17.

5. "A Survey of the New Media," *The Economist,* April 22, 2006, p. 15.

6. John Stossel, *Myths, Lies, and Downright Stupidity* (New York: Hyperion Press, 2006. pp. 4–6.)7

7. This particular usage of hypothesis has been noted extensively in accounts of the Battle of Midway. A good comprehensive account appears in Henry F. Schorreck, *Battle of Midway 4–7 June, 1942: The Role of Comint in the Battle of Midway*, at http://www.Historynavy.mil/faqs/faq81.

8. James Joyce, "Bayes Theorem," *The Stanford Encyclopedia of Philosophy (Winter 2003 Edition),* Edward N. Zalta, ed., URL (ed.), http://plato.stanford.edu/archives/win2003/entries, bayes-theorm/, p. 6.)

9. This brief account is drawn from Encyclopedia Britannica (online), the Concise Encyclopedia of Economics,and the Mind Tools website.

10. Douglas N. Walton, *Informal Logic: A Handbook for Critical Argumentation* (Cambridge, U. K.: Cambridge University Press, 1999), p. ix.

11. Ibid., p. x.

12. Shakespeare, *Macbeth* , V, v, 26–28.

13. Winston S. Churchill, *The Gathering Storm* (Boston: Houghton Mifflin Company, 1948), pp. 85, 168.

CHAPTER 5

1. Shakespeare, *Hamlet*, II, II. 316–323.

2. Roberta Wohlstetter, *Pearl Harbor:Warning and Decision*, (Stanford, California: Stanford University Press, 1962), p. 393.

3. Sophocles, *Oedipus Rex*, I, 872.

4. Shakespeare, *King Henry VIII, III, II,* 361–364.

5. Alexander Pope, *An Essay on Criticism*, II, I.

6. Shakespeare, *King Henry VIII,* III, II, 371–372.

7. Shakespeare, *Julius Caesar, I, II,* 136–150.

8. Sun Tzu, *The Art of War*, in Thomas R. Phillips, *Roots of Strategy* (Harrisburg, Pa.: Military Services Publishing Company, 1941), p. 28.

CHAPTER 6

1. *The Ethics of Aristotle: The Nicomachean Ethics* (Baltimore, Md.: Penguin Books, Inc. 1958), p. 25.

2. Confucius' significant comments and aphorisms were collected by his later followers into the *Analects*, which comprise the main body of Confucian thought. The quotations in this brief commentary on his work are drawn from Analects 12:1, 9:4, and 6:30.

3. Josef Pieper, *The Four Cardinal Virtues: Prudence, Justice, Fortitude, Temperance* (New York: Harcourt Brace and World, Inc., 1965). This work is based on four more extensive studies previously published: *Fortitude* and *Temperance,* 1954; *Justice,* 1955; *Prudence,* 1959.

4. Ibid., pp. 14–15. The remainder of this discussion derives from pp. 14–21.

5. Shakespeare, *Hamlet,* III, II, 74–79.

6. *Hamlet,* I, III, 59–80.

7. Socrates left no written works. The comment appears in Plato's *Apology, 38a.*

Selected Bibliography

Baron, J. *Thinking and Deciding.* Cambridge: Cambridge University Press, 1988.

Braverman, Jerome D. *Management Decision Making: a formal-intuitive approach.* New York, N.Y., AMACOM, 1998.

Churchill, Richard Todd. *Becoming a Critical Thinker: A Guide for the New Millennium.* Pearson Custom Publishing, 2000.

_____. *The Skeptic's Dictionary.* John Wiley and Sons, 2003.

Drucker, Peter F. *Managing for Results: economic tasks and risk-taking decisions.* New York: Harper and Row, 1964.

_____. *Management: Tasks, Responsibilities, Practices.* New York: Harper and Row, 1974.

_____. *The Effective Executive.* New York: Harper and Row, 1967.

Dunn, Robert A. *Management Science: a practical approach to decision making.* New York: Macmillan, 1981.

Flynn, Daniel J. *Intellectual Morons: How Ideology Makes Smart People Fall For Stupid Ideas.* New York, N.Y.: Crown Forum, 2004.

Gladwell, Malcolm. *Blink: The Power of Thinking Without Thinking.* New York, Boston: Little, Brown and Company, 2005.

Hammond, John S., Keeney, Ralph L., Raiffa, Howard. *Smart Choices A Practical Guide to Making Better Decisions.* Boston: Harvard Business School Press, 1999.

Harvard Business Review. *Harvard Business Review on Decision Making.* Boston: Harvard Business School Publishing Corporation, 2001.

Heller, Robert. *Essential Manager's Manual.* New York, N.Y.: DK Publishing, 1998.

Hoch, Stephen J., Kunreuther, Howard C., with Gunther, Robert E. *Wharton on Making Decisions.* New York: John Wiley & Sons, 2001.

Howard, V. A. *Thinking Together: Making Meetings Work.* New York: W. Morrow, 1992.

Janis, Irving L. and Mann, Leon. *Decision Making: A Psychological Analysis of Conflict, Choice and Commitment.* New York: The Free Press, 1977.

Jones, Morgan D. *The Thinker's Toolkit: Fourteen Skills for Making Smarter Decisions in Business and in Life.* New York: Times Business/Random House, 1995.

Jones, W. T.: Sontag, Frederick; Beckner, Morton O.; Fogelin, Robert J., eds. *Approaches to Ethics: Representative Selections from Classical Times to the Present.* 3rd. Ed. New York: McG raw Hill Book Company, 1977.

Kepner, Charles and Tregoe, Benjamin B. *The Rational Manager: A Systematic Approach to Problem Solving and Decision Making.* New York: McGraw Hill Book Company, 1965.

Klein, David and Klein, Marymae E. *How Do You Know It's True? Sifting Sense From Nonsense.* New York: Charles Scribner's Sons, 1984.

Pieper, Josef. *The Four Cardinal Virtues: Prudence, Justice, Fortitude, Temperance.* New York: Harcourt Brace and World, Inc., 1965.

Poundstone, William. *Fortune's Formula: the Untold Story of the Scientific Betting System That Beat Consensus and Wall Street.* New York: Hill and Wang, 2005.

Saaty, Thomas L. *Decision Making for Leaders: the Analytic Hierarchy Process for Decisions in a Complex World.* Pittsburgh, Pa.: R.S. Publications, 1990.

Siegel, Jeremy. *The Future for Investors: Why the Tried and True Triumphs Over the Bold and New.* New York: Crown Books, 2005.

Smith, Walter Bedell. *Eisenhower's Six Great Decisions (Europe, 1944–1945).* New York, London, Toronto. Longmans, Green and Co., 1956.

Stossel, John. *Myths, Lies, and Downright Stupidity.* New York: Hyperion, 2006.

Sun Tzu, The Art of War, in Phillips, Thomas R. *Roots of Strategy.* Harrisburg, Pa.: Military Service Publishing Company, 1940.

Sutherland, Norman Stuart. *Irrationality: Why we don't think straight.* New Brunswick, N. J.: Rutgers University Press, 1994.

Walton, Douglas. *Informal Logic: A Handbook for Critical Argumentation.* Cambridge: Cambridge University Press, 1993.

Wohlstetter, Roberta. *Pearl Harbor: Warning and Decision.* Stanford, Calif.: Stanford University Press, 1962.

Index